NEW ORLEANS

by Oliver Evans

THE MACMILLAN COMPANY

New York   1959

The Macmillan Company, New York
Brett-Macmillan Ltd., Galt, Ontario

Library of Congress catalog card number: 59-9948

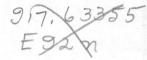

For Ardis Mayhew Blackburn

Author's note

I wish to thank the following persons, all of whom assisted in some way to the preparation of this book: Lynn Altenbernd, Elmo Avet, Mrs. Ardis Blackburn, Christopher S. Blake, Glen Douthit, Gilbert J. Fortier, Jr., Jack N. Fricks, Harry J. Gaeta, Charles J. Gill, William Gray, Lawrence Jennings, Jr., Aaron M. Kohn, Mrs. Lynnette Landry, J. Kearney Livaudais, William L. May, Martin Palmer, Bobbie Saucier, Mrs. Tom Sawyer, Clay Shaw, and Mrs. Luz Thomas. For their patience and cooperation I wish also to thank the staffs of the New Orleans Public Library, the University of Illinois Library, and the Louisiana State Museum.

Urbana, Illinois
May, 1959

Contents

Contents

Illustrations

ONE

In General

In General

No two places, obviously, are ever exactly alike, for places, like people, have lives of their own, and absolute duplication is impossible. But there are resemblances, and much of the excitement of visiting a new place consists in our being able to perceive these resemblances at the same time that we are aware of its uniqueness, of the special quality that distinguishes it from all other places we have ever visited. Sometimes the differences are more apparent than the similarities; when this is so, we are likely to say that the place is "interesting," by which, I think, we mean merely that it is unique.

Of the larger American cities, New Orleans is probably the most interesting in this sense. To say, as has been said so often, that it is like no other American city is true but misleading, for it implies that it is like some city outside the United States—some European city, for instance, and this is not the case. For though it is true that it resembles Lyons, on the Rhone, more than it does, say, Dallas, it is not really like either of those places. As it happens, the two cities which New Orleans most closely resembles are both in the New World, though far apart and very different each from the other: they are Quebec and Havana, but here again the differences are greater than the similarities.

No, New Orleans is unlike any other city anywhere else; like the local coffee, a dark roast flavored more or less discreetly with chicory, it has its special flavor, and the visitor is aware of it immediately. Atmosphere is to a place what personality is to an individual—few things are so difficult to analyze or define; you know it perhaps more by its absence than by its presence, and yet there are certain elements in the atmosphere of New Orleans by which nearly everyone is impressed.

There is first of all the light, with its peculiarly diaphanous quality, the result of a fine haze which the sun (though it is as fierce here as in Tucson or Miami) never quite succeeds in dispelling: there is thus, in spite of the frequently intense heat, little of the glare which characterizes those cities. The light is soft and subtle, with opalescent tints, and the dawns and dusks are peculiarly luminous. The air is heavy; you expect to see it liquefy at any moment, and of course it often does—umbrellas are in order the year round, though they are seldom used for more than a few minutes at a time. In the summer the average mean temperature is only about 84 degrees, but the relative humidity is as high as 77 per cent—which is about the maximum for any city, large or small, in the United States. In July and August the atmosphere resembles that of a steam room: you have only to walk a block or so before your shirt, however firmly it may have been starched, begins to soften and sag, and your trousers to lose their crease. Out of doors, at this time of year, no one is ever quite dry. Water is the city's natural element: it virtually surrounds it (the French colonists always referred to New Orleans as the Ile d'Orléans), and it is never very far from the surface of the earth. The city is actually below sea level, requiring an elaborate system of pumps and an intricate network of canals totaling 108 miles—longer than those of Venice.

The effect of so much sun and rain is to cause vegetation to flourish with a tropical luxuriance; in addition, the Mississippi Valley soil is remarkably rich and fertile. The city is like a giant hothouse. Plants spring up overnight and have to be constantly pruned and trimmed to keep them from taking over the entire property: one notices this especially in the so-called Garden District, where the yards are biggest and greenest—if given half a chance, the foliage would swallow up the houses. In vacant lots the weeds grow as high as a man's head, and on the walls of the older brick houses, where the mortar has fallen out in places, you will see ferns and even miniature trees sprouting; in the cemeteries, abandoned mausoleums have been split open in this way—burials here, owing to the aqueous nature of the soil, are all above ground. Your shoes will mildew overnight in really damp weather unless your room happens to be air conditioned, and in no other city has air conditioning proved such a blessing: everyone who can afford a unit buys one; it is as necessary here as is a good furnace in Minnesota.

AERIAL VIEW OF NEW ORLEANS

VIEW FROM FRENCH QUARTER BALCONY

Then there is the architecture, or rather the architectures, for there are at least half a dozen salient styles: in this respect New Orleans is certainly the most interesting city in the United States. The French Quarter alone, a relatively small area of eight by fourteen blocks, contains hundreds of houses, almost any one of which, elsewhere in the country, would perhaps be set aside as a state monument. Here they are so numerous that they are taken for granted, and the natives in particular seldom notice them, seldom really *see* them—as is, I suppose, always and almost necessarily the case. There are two distinct types, cottage and mansion, the former usually French, or rather Colonial French; the latter, Spanish. The cottages antedate the mansions; they are one- and one-and-a-half-story affairs, primitively but strongly constructed of brick sometimes covered with stucco, with overhanging eaves and roofs sloping rather sharply to the front and rear. The mansions are larger and more refined, two and sometimes three stories tall, with balconies on which the ornamental iron grilles are often (but by no means always) very beautiful. Both cottages and mansions face directly on the street; the yards, or rather courtyards, are to the rear, in the Spanish manner—they are private affairs with high walls and, usually, a fountain. Opposite the main house, and separated from it by the courtyard, is the slave quarter, a simple two-story building of the same width as the house but only one room deep.

These houses look indescribably ancient. Actually the oldest of them are no earlier than the latter part of the eighteenth century, but they look as old as the houses of Pompeii. New England houses of the same date, and earlier, have nothing of the weatherbeaten quality that these have, and of course the New England weather is much harsher. The truth is that everything in New Orleans looks much older than it is, as J. B. Priestley, the English novelist, pointed out in one of the most perceptive articles ever written about the city (*Harper's*, May, 1938). In five years a house will look as if it had stood there for fifty; it will have a look of having settled ever so slightly into the moist earth, of having endured innumerable alternations of rain and sun, and of having been gently and gradually caressed for generations by the fine fingers of fungi. Within, dampness causes the plaster to peel off in a matter of months—homeowners are always experimenting with mixes to find one that is really waterproof, but no one ever quite seems to succeed.

Some of the French Quarter houses are in a shocking state of neglect, with sagging roofs and great leprous-looking patches on the walls where the cement has fallen away, revealing the bare brick beneath. Restoring them can be a fascinating business, but it is enormously difficult and far more expensive than you might suppose—a hobby for millionaires. Whole fortunes have been sunk into such ventures, and the amateur of ordinary means who wants a house in New Orleans will be wise either to build new (though this is forbidden in the French Quarter except by permission of the Vieux Carré Commission) or, if he is determined upon an old house, to buy one which has already been restored.

Elsewhere in the city, especially in the Garden District, you will notice another type of old house which belongs to a later period—the prosperous 1840's and 1850's, just before the Civil War. These are more grandiose, larger even than the largest Spanish mansions, and are built of wood almost invariably painted white: the style is Greek Revival, modified, particularly in the later buildings, with Gothic overtones. They are set off some distance from the street in a yard which is usually surrounded by an iron fence or wall, sometimes a wall of shrubbery, and are also equipped with slave quarters and carriage houses.

These buildings are not very different from the ante-bellum mansions you will see in Natchez. The interiors are frequently magnificent, with elaborate wedding-cake moldings, marble fireplaces, full-length built-in mirrors, and dazzling chandeliers. They have not been tampered with as have the older French Quarter houses, where it is often difficult to distinguish the original effect from that created fifty years later by a restoration, and to distinguish *that* effect from a still later one: everything here looks almost equally old after a few years. But these houses, many of them, look exactly as they did upon completion, except, of course, for the electrical fixtures and an occasional air-conditioning unit laboring away at a tremendous disadvantage in rooms of such gigantic proportions. The wealthier families in New Orleans live in such houses—the *nouveaux riches* excepted, whom you will find mostly in Metairie. The slave quarters make ideal guest houses, and the carriage houses have been converted into garage apartments for the servants.

A third type of house that you will notice is the Victorian cottage, with its fantastic gingerbread façade and colored glass windows; the larger houses will be complete with cupolas and turrets, with, indoors, an effect of paneled walls and airless, gloomy corridors. These are scattered pretty much all over town, except in the newest sections, and in few cities will you find such flamboyant examples of this extraordinary style. Victorian houses are enjoying a certain vogue at the moment: looking at these samples, you are rather glad of it, for, absurd as they often are and as little as you might like to live in one, you could not really wish them out of existence.

There are many who think of New Orleans in terms of food. New Orleans food is not typically Southern, any more than the city itself is: if you are looking for fried chicken, corn bread or beaten biscuits, buttermilk, mustard greens with plenty of pot liquor, stewed corn, blackberry cobbler, and the like, you will have to go up toward Shreveport, near the Arkansas line, or to the northeast in the direction of Mississippi—say Vicksburg or Natchez. The local dishes are relatively highly seasoned, with less emphasis on vegetables and more on the *pièces de résistance* and the sauces with which they are served. Seafood from the Gulf of Mexico and Lake Pontchartrain (which, being connected to the Gulf, is semisalt) is ubiquitous. The most popular fish are flounder, pompano, and redfish, and there are lots of shrimp, crabs, and oysters. Louisiana oysters are among the largest anywhere; they are as big as the Maryland variety, though not so flavorsome as the smaller ones found along the west coast of Florida.

New Orleans cooking, or Creole cooking, as it is sometimes called, is hybrid and unique. Basically it is French, and more particularly southern French, for many of the herbs and spices grown in Louisiana had been at home also in the warm region of the Côte d'Azur—but not all of them, like the *gumbo filé*, a pungent herb cultivated by the Indians and used by them in their stews. It did not take Colonial cooking long to distinguish itself from that of the mother country as it became modified, first by Indian, later by Spanish and even African influences. It is interesting to compare Louisiana cooking with French Canadian, which is not French either, though closer to it (and particularly to the Norman and Breton cuisines) than is the Creole: the Canadian is much simpler and much blander.

The result of all this tradition has been to make New Orleans the only American city of any size whose inhabitants have developed a genuinely sophisticated palate. I know of no other city in this country where you can be reasonably sure of eating well in restaurants chosen at random. Such a situation would not, perhaps, be phenomenal in a French or Italian city, but here it is unparalleled. Even in the most unpretentious places there is an acknowledgment of the importance of good food well served; it reveals itself in a number of little ways, such as the action of a waitress in running scalding water over a cup before she fills it with coffee, so that it will remain hot. A restaurant in New Orleans *has* to be good in order to stay in business, for the natives take their food seriously, and there is a great deal of competition.

Like most cities with a definite atmosphere, New Orleans has certain characteristic sounds and odors. You cannot spend much time in the downtown area without becoming aware, delightfully, of the odor of roasting coffee: this is the coffee center of the United States. There is also the heavy, sweet smell of malt from the breweries, two of which, Jax and Regal, are located in the French Quarter, and there are times when the whole area smells like a gigantic taproom. Upper Royal Street is fragrant with perfume and sachet shops; there is a lively market for the local essences, magnolia and jasmine particularly, and for the aromatic vetiver root, which is used, like lavender, to sweeten the drawers of clothes presses. Only a few blocks away, by contrast, are the fish and poultry stenches along Decatur Street and in the French Market; on the wharves the sharp odors of green bananas and mahogany logs from Central America mingle with exciting tar and rope smells. The uptown gardens are odorous with magnolia, Cape jasmine and honeysuckle; there are the marvelous scents of the sweet olive, too (like that of ripe apricots), and of night-blooming jasmine—heady, almost sickly-sweet, and overpowering in the evening all the other odors of the neighborhood.

As for sounds, the one I think most typical is the penetrating, low-pitched, rather mournful blast of steamships on the river: you are apt to hear it at any hour of the day or night, though of course more frequently when the weather is foggy. It reminds you, if you need reminding, that you are in a port, and actually it is no more typical of New Orleans than it is of New York or San Francisco; but in those cities, because of their size, you are not so conscious of it. The street cries of New Orleans used to be famous, but they are fast disappearing: the chimney sweeps are heard no more, the knife grinders and charcoal vendors but seldom, and the mulatto women calling "*Calas tout chauds*" have been gone for half a century. But you can still hear an occasional Negro on a creaking wagon chanting "Blaaack-ber-ries" or "Ba-naaa-nas" or "Waaat-er-mel-ons," depending upon the season, in a sleepy, plaintively prolonged voice, or the monotonous recitative: "I got fresh corn, eggplants, butterbeans, cantaloupe, okra, tomatoes . . ."

All of these things make for a certain individuality, yet I believe that what most distinguishes the city of my birth from other American cities is the people. New Orleans is the only large city in the country whose inhabitants *look* at one another on the street. New York, for instance, is like a city of highly animated somnambulists: no one, unless he has special motives, really notices anybody else. The pace at which the inhabitants move about is one reason; it precludes observation, as it precludes reflection, but it is not the principal one. New Yorkers are incurious, as are Chicagoans; they do not really care who you are or what you look like. This is of course a defensive attitude: in cities of such size, almost the only way in which the individual can maintain his identity is by excluding others from his notice. Yet it is, or can be, rather frightening.

Here, on the other hand, everyone is aware of everyone else. People do not attempt, as happens sometimes in small towns, to mind one another's business; the place is too big for that, yet it is not so big as to breed indifference. There is a respect for individuality, and, as yet, plenty of room for it. (I say "as yet" because the city is growing so very fast.) Idiosyncrasies flourish as do the plants, and sometimes, like the plants, they run riot: the city is full of "characters"; few of them, however, are offensive, many are entertaining, and nearly all of them are interesting in one way or another.

An attitude such as this makes for tolerance, by no means the poorest of civic virtues, and New Orleanians have plenty of it— more than their share, perhaps, for tolerance can result in decadence, and there is plenty of that too. New Orleans has often been called the wickedest of American cities, and I suppose that, in a sense, it is. But its sins are more of the flesh than of the will, of impulse rather than of calculation. Lust is more in evidence than greed, and lust, as everyone knows, is not always unmixed with love. However serious the city's vices, they are always profoundly human, and, as in the case of an individual, oddly blended with its virtues.

A Latin morality is the city's heritage, and Latin morality was originally a pagan morality—the morality of ancient Rome, a very different business from the morality of Roman Catholicism which superseded it (while retaining certain features) and more different still from that of the Protestant reformers, Luther, Calvin, Wesley, *et al.*, none of whom ever found really significant following in the Latin countries. New Orleans presents the phenomenon of a Latin, Roman Catholic culture (there are nearly three times as many Catholics here as members of all other religions combined) surrounded by a culture which is primarily Anglo-Saxon and Protestant; its morality is not that of Memphis or Denver. I suppose the climate, too, contributes partly to the paganism of the place: certainly Calvinism of the New England variety could never have taken root in this luxuriant semitropical soil, and the young men and women here mature somewhat earlier than they do in the Northern cities—one reason, perhaps, for the rather high rate of juvenile delinquency. There is a strong atmosphere of sexuality overhanging the entire city; it is strongest, of course, in the French Quarter, a neighborhood now dedicated (like Greenwich Village, only more so) to bohemianism and night life, but you are conscious of it everywhere. It has always been so. "Great Babylon is come up before me," wrote Andrew Jackson's wife, Rachel, during a visit here. "Oh the wickedness, the idolatry of this place. Oh farewell. Pray for your sister in a heathen land."

New Orleanians are a pleasure-loving people generally, and it is the simpler pleasures of which they are fondest: love-making, eating, drinking, dancing, and going to the movies. Everyone wants to have a good time, and the worst fate that can possibly befall a native is to be bored. He will spend more on entertainment than will the inhabitants of most other cities; amusement must be achieved at any cost, even at the cost of going into debt, and the theaters, restaurants, cabarets, and loan companies do a thriving business. He will also spend more on transportation: no one will walk five blocks if he has the price of a bus fare in his pocket—and the fare (seven cents) is lower here than in any other city in the United States. In this respect New Orleanians of French descent differ strongly from their country cousins, descendants of the thrifty Canadian farmers who migrated to Louisiana in 1764 and 1765 after their expulsion by the British from what is now Nova Scotia: these, known as *Acadiens* (corrupted to *Cajuns*), settled mainly to the west of the Mississippi, forming villages which developed into the present towns of Opelousas, Lafayette, New Iberia, Ville Platte, Thibodaux, Houma and St. Martinville, and are notorious for their acquisitiveness and penny pinching.

The natives are apt to be extravagant in the matter of dress, too; there is a concern for appearance that is peculiarly Gallic. Strolling casually along Canal Street, you will be surprised at the number of well groomed men and women; the latter are particularly elegant, and it is not always because they are wearing expensive clothes. You will also be surprised at their vivacity. They will talk for the pure pleasure of talking, and their gestures will remind you of southern Europeans. Their speech is considerably faster than that of Atlantans, for example, or Houstonians, and they move about, in spite of the heat, with more animation than do the natives of other cities in the Deep South. No one appears to be in a seriously bad humor: the natives lose their tempers easily but recover them just as easily, and it is usually over little, momentary things—a selfish motorist, for instance, or a jaywalker. Large-scale resentments are rare, and you will seldom see an exhibition of really bad manners. New Orleanians are generally polite, and relations between the sexes still have something of the slightly ritualistic quality of a Mediterranean culture: the men are inclined to flatter the women outrageously, make a show of catering to their every whim, and stare at them boldly on the street—exactly as in Rome or Naples. The women are not deceived by all of this; they do not mistake it for sincerity, and are, if anything, somewhat quicker than most American women at distinguishing a passing interest from a serious one: they have had more experience with *galanterie*, and they accept it for what it is—a ritual, one of the mores. But it is not unpleasing.

All this Latinity is the more surprising when you reflect that only a very small percentage of the population of the modern city is of French and Spanish origin. No one knows exactly how many Creoles (as the descendants of the early colonists are called) there are in the city today, but there are fewer than you would guess unless you knew something of the city's populational history. When New Orleans was acquired from France by the United States in 1803, its population, black and white, was 10,000. Twenty years later it had grown to more than three times that number, and the newcomers were mainly of Anglo-Saxon stock, migrants from the Middle Western and Allegheny regions. Today it stands at 640,000 (779,000 if you include the suburban area), and, after the many nineteenth century waves of European immigration, is about as hybrid as any American population could well be: the Irish and Italian colonies are particularly large, and in the 1850's the number of Germans here was large enough to justify the publication of a daily newspaper in that language, the *Täglische Deutsche Zeitung.* Nevertheless, it is the original population, a potent one culturally as well as biologically, which has triumphed over succeeding ones and given to the present generation of New Orleanians, of whatever origin, most of the characteristics which distinguish them from the inhabitants of other American cities.

For all their worldliness, the natives exhibit (as Priestley noted) a curious provincialism. They are interested in other people, but not in other places: like the natives of many tourist centers, they do not have to go to the world; the world has come to them. There is nothing they haven't seen or heard, right here in New Orleans—or so they think, at any rate. This complacency is most pronounced where you would, perhaps, least expect to find it: in the city's upper classes. The local society is extraordinarily self-sufficient. It is not unlikely for a New York millionaire to have a summer place in Canada, or a country home in Florida, but New Orleans millionaires are not like that. Only a few of them own houses elsewhere—across the lake, usually, in Covington or Mandeville, but no farther. It is not a point of conscience with them to have been to Paris or the Riviera, nor to have seen the latest Broadway plays.

A discerning acquaintance of mine, a European gentleman who had visited every major city in the United States, once told me he thought the outstanding quality of New Orleanians was their *softness*. He intended it, I think, as a compliment; in any case it is an interesting observation. He was referring mainly to their manners, and a less sympathetic observer (a New Englander or Middle Westerner, for instance) might have called it insincerity rather than softness, for a typical native will prefer to tell you an untruth rather than run the risk of offending you by saying something which, though true, might conceivably give offense. Everything about the place, he noted, was soft—even the water, and it is true that you will not find softer water anywhere. The local speech, modified by so many Mediterranean influences, is softer than that of most Southerners, except possibly South Carolinians, and is almost entirely free from drawl. One of its peculiarities is the tendency to pronounce *first* and *third* like *foist* and *thoid*, in an effort to avoid the harsh *r* sound—just as in Brooklyn, though not so obviously, and there are other resemblances to Brooklynese in the local pronunciation, a circumstance which, though it has impressed many, I have never seen satisfactorily explained.

Hedonistic, complacent, extravagant where amusement is concerned, soft to the point sometimes of insincerity, tolerant to the point sometimes of decadence; but always vivacious, good-natured, well dressed and well mannered—these are the characteristics of a typical New Orleanian. You might think, perhaps, that his vices outweigh his virtues; it depends on what you believe is important, but there is no denying that he is an easy fellow to get along with. It *is* a pity he is not more serious. New Orleans is probably the least intellectual city of any size in America: there are surprisingly few bookshops, a situation which has existed ever since the days of Colonial occupation. Berquin-du-Vallon noted in 1803 that there were no booksellers in the city, "and for a good reason, that a bookseller would perish of hunger there in the midst of his books, unless these taught the fascinated reader the art of doubling his capital in a year's time." The more serious plays, when they come here on tour, perform almost invariably to half-empty houses. It is much the same with music. There was a genuine operatic tradition here in the nineteenth century, when the French Opera House on the corner of Bourbon and Toulouse streets was one of the finest on the hemisphere, but it died out in 1914, when the theater gave its last performance, and has never been revived. The building burned to the ground in 1919. Not until comparatively recent years was there a Philharmonic Society worthy of the name; in this respect the city lagged far behind others in America. As for painting, in spite of much activity, there is unfortunately very little that is first rate. As is so often the case with places strong on atmosphere (Provincetown, Nantucket, Taos, Carmel, San Miguel de Allende, and so on), New Orleans seems mainly to attract raffish bohemians with more temperament than talent, or facile water-colorists with a picture-postcard sense of the aesthetic. The French Quarter is swarming with café and sidewalk artists, particularly around Jackson Square; they will do your portrait (or that of your favorite movie star, copied from a photograph) in fifteen minutes flat, charcoal or pastel. The Delgado Museum, in City Park, has had for many years an undistinguished collection (copies and inferior Americana mostly), but it has recently been enriched by a permanent loan from the Samuel H. Kress Foundation. The building, however—a most attractive one—is nearly always empty.

No, New Orleans is a good-time town, and the overnight tourist's impression of it, based on a visit to the Bourbon Street honky-tonks, does not really miss the mark very widely: as a symbol, Bourbon Street has a certain accuracy. The city comes by this tradition legitimately; it was famous for its fleshpots as early as the middle of the eighteenth century, when the Marquis de Vaudreuil, who succeeded Bienville as Governor of Louisiana, drew up a set of articles designed to curb the vice which flourished along the waterfront and which threatened to demoralize the colony. Now, instead, it flourishes along Bourbon Street, after a number of shifts: first to Tchoupitoulas Street, then to Girod Street, then to Gallatin Street, then to Basin Street, then to the part of town known throughout America as Storyville, which lay mostly in the French Quarter. Gambling, a favorite vice of the Creoles, has now mostly been relegated to Jefferson Parish (the counties in Louisiana are known as parishes, for the basis on which the state was originally divided up was a religious one), where, though officially outlawed, it continues a surreptitious but active existence, and the notorious red-light district between North Rampart and Basin has been disorganized since the thirties, when Huey Long broke the power of the New Orleans politicians who controlled it. But it is only a fifteen-minute ride from Canal Street to Jefferson Parish, and almost any cab driver will take you to one of the many brothels which, instead of being confined to the district, are now scattered, for better or for worse, throughout the city. The more obvious forms of sex perversion are everywhere: if the homosexual element were to remove itself from the city, the population of the French Quarter would be decimated. Lotteries, though against the law, still exist, and horse racing, which has the status of a sport rather than the game of chance which it also is, enjoys an enormous legitimate popularity: when the season comes around, hardly anyone is immune. Everywhere you look you will see bars; both sides of Bourbon Street are lined almost solidly with them for a distance of ten blocks, and many stay open around the clock: it is without doubt the wettest city in America. Such was the corruption of the local police department that in 1953 a group of prominent citizens who had incorporated themselves independently as an impartial fact-finding group requested a probe from the outside, and Aaron M. Kohn, a Philadelphia attorney who was formerly one of J. Edgar Hoover's administrative assistants in the Training Schools Division of the F.B.I., came to the city for this purpose. Needless to say, he met with fierce opposition, but as a result of his disclosures the police department underwent a top-to-bottom shake-up.

Gambling, B-drinking, vice, and graft are the most conspicuous types of lawbreaking in New Orleans today, as they have always been, and of course they are closely related. They are the result of a tradition, and traditions are not easily effaced. Lottery gambling, in particular, has always had a special appeal in Latin countries; in most of them it is legalized, as it was in Louisiana in the period immediately following the Civil War, when the state itself sold tickets to finance the task of reconstruction. But crime generally is on the increase in New Orleans, as it is elsewhere in the nation, only here the rate of increase is somewhat higher and fewer criminals are apprehended: in 1958, less than one out of every five major crimes resulted in an arrest.

Mr. Kohn and the Crime Commission have accomplished a great deal of good: in some respects their work can be compared to that of the Vigilantes, a group of citizens who, outraged by dishonest voting practices during the corrupt Waterman administration in 1858, forced the mayor's resignation by seizing the Cabildo and holding it by force of arms against his henchmen. Instead of strong-arm tactics, however, they have used legal ones—though the legality of Mr. Kohn's information-gathering methods has been the subject of much local controversy, and that gentleman even received a short jail term, which he served stoically, for refusing to identify his informants. The task which they face is a tremendous one, for any reforms in a city dedicated, like this one, to the pleasure principle, are almost certain to be temporary—as were those of the Vigilantes. New Orleans has always been the despair of moralists: this, indeed, is one of the few aspects of the city which has not changed with the passing of years, and which does not seem likely to change in the future. For many of the characteristics I have mentioned, both of the city and the people, are disappearing—and disappearing fast. In another fifty or seventy-five years they will have disappeared forever, and then New Orleans, except for Bourbon Street (or the street which succeeds it and substitutes its function) will be indistinguishable from any other city in the South—and, in time, from any other city in the United States, for the differences between the South and the rest of the country are disappearing, too, though more slowly and imperceptibly. Populationally the city has mushroomed in the last decade, and there is every indication that it will continue to grow, particularly in the suburban areas: the newcomers bring with them new mores, new mannerisms, new attitudes to life, and these are certain to exert a leveling influence. One by one the old houses are being torn down all over town except in the French Quarter, where they are protected by the Vieux Carré Commission, and it is rarely that you hear French spoken in the city nowadays; fifty years ago, in the French Quarter, it was almost as common as English. Nowadays New Orleanians *have* birthdays; they don't *make* them ("He made twenty yesterday"). The Negro marching bands, in which the great jazz pioneers like Louis Armstrong and Sidney Bechet received their early training, are becoming increasingly rare, and coffee and gumbo are no longer sold in the cemeteries on All Saints' Day, when New Orleanians decorate their graves. The food is still good, probably the best in America, but even it is not as good as it was, for the local palate is being vitiated daily by the drugstores and the cafeterias. Good food takes time to prepare, as it takes time to enjoy, and everyone nowadays is in such a hurry: in most restaurants, leisurely dining is very nearly a thing of the past. Until recently (the end of World War II, I think), a man or a boy would have blushed to remain seated in a streetcar while a woman was standing in it, and streetcar manners are still better here, as are manners generally, than in New York or Chicago—but that is beginning to change, too, and soon it will be, as in those cities, a matter of first come, first served.

In the meantime, New Orleans remains a most pleasant place to live in, except perhaps in midsummer, and an exciting place to visit. It may shock, exasperate, even seriously annoy you for a while, but you cannot, unless you are a Savonarola, be permanently angry with New Orleans. And even if you were a Savonarola, predicting in the marketplace the destruction of the city for its sins, you would not be burned for it: the natives would listen to you politely enough, then decide a movie was more amusing. They might even ask you to come along.

TWO

Backgrounds

What! Is it expected that, for any commercial or profitable purpose, boats will ever be able to run up the Mississippi, into the Wabash, the Missouri, or the Red River? One might as well try to bite a slice off the moon.

—La Mothe Cadillac, fifth Governor of Louisiana, in a letter to the Court of Louis XIV (1714)

Backgrounds

❧ OLD as it is, New Orleans is not as old as a number of other cities in the Deep South—some of the Spanish settlements antedate it by over a hundred years. The little town of Biloxi, on the Mississippi Gulf Coast, now a favorite summer resort with New Orleanians, was founded in 1699 by Pierre le Moyne, Sieur de Iberville, nearly twenty years before New Orleans; it is one of the very few surviving seventeenth century settlements in the Delta region, and was the first capital of the colony. (Louisiana at that time included the entire territory between the Illinois River on the north and the Gulf of Mexico on the south, and between the English colonies on the east and the Spanish possessions on the west.) Mississippians still like to remind their western neighbors that the first two capitals of Louisiana were towns in Mississippi, and Alabamans are no less backward in pointing out that Louisiana's third capital was Mobile, founded in 1702 by Jean Baptiste le Moyne, Sieur de Bienville, who was Iberville's brother. Iberville and Bienville were Canadians, members of a prominent Quebec family which had been raised to petty nobility by Louis XIV. New Orleans was founded in 1718 by Bienville, who had long been aware of the advantages of its location, but it was not to become the capital for four more years: in 1719, when it became necessary to shift the seat of government once more, it was passed over in favor of New Biloxi, on the east side of Biloxi Bay and only a few miles from the site of the first capital.

Bienville, though probably the first, was not the only man to perceive the potential value of the site of New Orleans. Father Charlevoix, the Jesuit historian and missionary who came to Louisiana

19

in the early eighteenth century, expressed confidence in the city's future in 1720, in a letter to the Duchess of Lesdiguières. "You will ask me, Madame," he added, "upon what I base this hope? I base it upon the situation of the city at thirty-three leagues from the sea; upon the bank of a navigable river by which the city may be reached in twenty-four hours; upon the fertility of its soil; upon its proximity to Mexico which can be reached in fifteen days; upon that to Havana which is even nearer; upon that to the most beautiful islands of America and to the English colonies." It is true that this letter was written before Father Charlevoix had visited Louisiana, and that when he arrived in New Orleans, a year or so later, his immediate reaction was one of disillusionment, but, as it turned out, the prophet viewed the city from a distance more truly than did the man inside it with his own eyes—one of the many small ironies of history, and time has shown Father Charlevoix's original prediction to have been almost uncannily accurate: the situation of New Orleans on a great river, at only a few miles from its estuary, established for it the dual identity of river port and seaport (the obvious analogy with Quebec probably did not escape either the priest or Bienville); the fertility of the Mississippi Valley soil is fabulous; and at this moment commerce with the Latin American countries is one of New Orleans' greatest economic assets.

Two years after Father Charlevoix wrote his letter, the fact that New Orleans could be made into a seaport was dramatically demonstrated by the engineers Blondel de la Tour and Adrien de Pauger (who first laid out the streets of the city) when they passed safely over the bar of the Mississippi in their ship, appropriately named *Aventurier*, on July 2, 1722. De la Tour wrote that he found fourteen feet of water in the channel, and added: "In going up the river, I examined the best place to establish New Orleans. I did not find a better situation than the place where it already is; not only is the land higher, but it is near a bayou, which is a little river, which falls into Lake Pontchartrain, through which one can at all times communicate with the New Biloxi, Mobile, and other ports, more easily than by the mouth of the river." De la Tour's report is interesting for two reasons: it shows the importance which the early colonists attached to the fact that large ships could come up the river and moor at the city's dock (at Biloxi the water was so shallow they had to anchor offshore), and it also shows that inland water communication with other colonial settlements was a decisive factor in the early growth of New Orleans.

Pauger, who planned the new city, divided it into sixty-six squares, the first row of which extended horizontally along the river and contained a *place* in its center. Each settler was given a lot 260 feet deep with a frontage of 130 feet; these were enclosed with palisades and surrounded by drainage ditches. Each square was also surrounded by a larger ditch, or moat, so that the city looked like a rustic Venice. Drainage was a problem from the first, particularly as the Mississippi overflowed its banks regularly every spring, and the first levees were constructed not under the supervision of Governor Etienne de Périer in 1727, as is commonly thought, but (as Alcée Fortier has shown in his *History of Louisiana*) by a moat-digger named Joseph Dubreuil, who by 1724, during Bienville's administration, had already built a system of primitive dikes.

The city was called New Orleans in honor of the Duke of Orléans, who was Regent of France; and the streets were named chiefly for various princes, dukes, and counts in the mother country (Bourbon, Orléans, Burgundy, Conti, Chartres, Toulouse, Du Maine) and for certain popular saints (St. Louis, St. Peter, St. Ann). Bienville, founder of the city, was honored by having a street named after him, and the Ursuline Sisters (a group of whom came to New Orleans in 1727) were likewise honored; Ursuline Street, however, was originally called St. Adrian. As the years passed, other streets came to be named after important buildings located on them, or for their contemporary function, like Customhouse (later changed to Iberville); Barracks, where military troops were quartered; Esplanade, where the same troops paraded; Rampart, which was a fortification defending the rear of the city; and Canal, which was the moat constituting the (southeastern) boundary. One entered and left the city by means of large gates, which were closed at nine o'clock.

The first settlers were an ill-assorted collection of Canadian *aventuriers des bois* and Frenchmen of all conditions, lured to Louisiana by the glowing descriptions of it circulated in France by the government of Louis XIV in an effort to populate the new colony. Louisiana at this time was controlled on a charter basis by a commercial enterprise known as the Company of the West and of the Indies (also known as the Mississippi Company), the president of which was that extraordinary financial schemer John Law. This company, backed by the French regent, possessed a monopoly on all French trade with Asia, Africa, and America and was also, for all practical purposes, exclusive owner of the entire Mississippi Valley. Investing money in such a venture seemed to many Frenchmen who had never been any farther from home than Paris or London (and even to many who had) a sure way of getting rich quickly. Louisiana was said to be full of gold and silver mines, and everyone who could raise the money bought shares. Between 1718 and 1720 France was seized by a wave of collective hysteria absolutely without precedent in its economic history: in order to obtain cash, noblemen mortgaged and even sold outright estates which had been in the possession of their families for centuries. "Quincampoix Street, where the offices of the company were kept," writes Charles Gayarré, dean of Louisiana historians, "was literally blocked up by the crowd which the fury of speculation and the passion for sudden wealth attracted to that spot, and persons were frequently crushed or stifled to death. 'Mississippi!—who wants any Mississippi?'—was bawled out in every lane and by-lane, and every nook and corner of Paris echoed with the word, 'Mississippi!' " There was of course little or no sound basis for speculation on such a scale, and when the "Mississippi Bubble" finally broke, its consequences were such as to make it one of the most tragical events in the history of eighteenth century France.

But even at the height of its prestige, the Mississippi Company found that it was easier to sell shares than to colonize the new territory, and colonization was a necessity if the imagined wealth of Louisiana was ever to be realized. All kinds of inducements were offered to prospective colonists, and, when these did not supply the demand, the inmates of prisons and brothels were exported en masse. Citizens from lower walks of life were frequently shanghaied and sent to Louisiana: under a monarchy as almost Orientally absolute as that of *le Roi Soleil*, such things were only too possible, the more so as the Mississippi Company enjoyed the backing of the Crown, and Louis XIV was determined to exploit the colony as quickly as possible in order to finance his wars and court extravagances. The situation provided the Abbé Prévost with the theme for his novel *Manon Lescaut*, the heroine of which has been abducted in this manner, and the novel in its turn supplied both Massenet and Puccini with operatic inspiration.

To put it mildly, the quality of the earliest settlers in New Orleans thus left much to be desired. As early as 1703, fifteen years before the founding of the city, Iberville had complained to the home government: "It is necessary to send here honest tillers of the soil, and not rogues and paupers, who come to Louisiana solely with the intention of making a fortune, by all sorts of means, in order to speed back to Europe. Such men cannot be elements of prosperity to a colony." And in 1714 Antoine de la Mothe Cadillac, who was Louisiana's fifth governor and also the founder of Detroit, wrote disgustedly, after observing that Louisiana was a "very wretched country": "The inhabitants are no better than the country; they are the very scum and refuse of Canada, ruffians who have thus far cheated the gibbet of its due, vagabonds who are without subordination to the laws, without any respect for religion or for the government, graceless profligates, who are so steeped in vice that they prefer the Indian females to the French women!" He went on to say bitterly: "Believe me, this whole continent is not worth having, and our colonists are so dissatisfied that they are all disposed to run away."

There were two reasons for the colonists' preferring Indian to French women: the depraved character of the latter as well as the fact that there were not enough to go around; when Cadillac was urged by missionaries to expel loose women from the colony, he replied: "I have refused to do so because if I sent away all women of loose habits, there would be no females left, and this would not suit the views of the government." In order to help remedy this situation, the home government sent over a number of girls of good family and of marriageable age, each equipped with a chest containing a small wardrobe: they were known as *filles à la cassette* (casket girls); the first of them came to New Orleans in 1728, and they continued to arrive until the middle of the century.

Cadillac's disillusionment was the common experience of many whom the glowing reports of Louisiana circulated in print and by word of mouth had not prepared for the harsh reality which awaited them on their arrival. Father Charlevoix, whose early optimism we have already noted, wrote disappointedly when he reached New Orleans three years after Bienville first cleared off its site: "The eight hundred beautiful houses in the five parishes which *Le Mercure* described two years ago are limited to a hundred huts placed without much order; to a large store built of wood; to two or three houses which would not adorn a French village; to the half of a wretched warehouse which the people willingly lent to the Lord and of which He had barely taken possession before they wanted to drive Him forth to lodge Him in a tent."

The hardships faced by the early colonists were such as to discourage all but the hardiest and most resolute. Accustomed to the mild climate of France and Canada, they suffered first of all from the peculiarly enervating heat of the New Orleans summer. Then there were the mosquitoes, and the yellow fever and malaria of which they were the carriers; the floods already referred to; the constant danger of attacks by Indians; and famine. Corn, which had been cultivated by the Indians, was the only staple which grew in any abundance, and the French (who used it at home for cattle) came to loathe it— particularly the women. Bienville wrote in one of his dispatches: "The males in the colony begin, through habit, to be reconciled to corn, as an article of nourishment; but the females, who are mostly Parisians, have for this kind of food a dogged aversion, which has not yet been subdued."

The Mississippi Company encouraged experiments with other crops, and as most of the settlers had neither an aptitude nor a liking for agricultural work, it began to export slaves from Africa to serve as field hands; these were sold to the colonists on credit. In 1721, three years after the founding of New Orleans, there were almost half as many slaves in the colony as white men—523, as against a total population, including some fifty Indians, of 1,256. This proportion created certain problems which led Bienville to draw up a body of laws known as the *Code Noir*, according to which whites were forbidden to marry Negroes or to have them for concubines. Apparently there was rigid enforcement of these laws in the early years of the French domination, as an English resident observed in a letter written in 1751: "They [the French] wisely prohibited, in the beginning, all marriages of whites with the savages, the Negroes or mulattoes, which has always been exactly observed since, so that one may say that the blood in that respect is as pure as in any kingdom in Europe, and very different from several other countries and colonies, particularly of the Spaniards, where one sees a horrible mixture of all races."

But though there was little racial mixture in eighteenth century Louisiana, there was much mixing of nationalities: New Orleans was America's first melting pot. All the principal countries of western Europe were represented, thanks to the effectiveness of John Law's propaganda. A group of German farmers settled about thirty miles up the river from what were then the city limits, at a spot which came to be known as the German Coast, where, through their industry and frugality, they prospered to such an extent that their settlement, about a hundred years later, was renamed the Gold Coast. The Germans were quick to intermarry with the French, and they readily absorbed the language and customs of their neighbors. A number of well known French names in New Orleans today are really of German origin: thus, Troxler was changed to Trosclair; Wichner to Vicknair; Huber to Oubre; Hummel to Hymel; and the ubiquitous Schexnayders derive their name from Jake Schneider, an Alsatian immigrant.

It was a German settler who left what is perhaps the earliest description of the city. Two years after its founding, he wrote: "I betook myself to where they are beginning the capital, New Orleans. Its circumference is one mile. The houses are poor and low, as with us at home in the country. They are covered with bark and reeds. Everyone dresses as he pleases but all very poorly. One's outfit consists of a suit of clothes, bed, table, and trunk. The people sleep the whole night in the open air. I am as safe in the more distant part of town as in a citadel. Although I live among savages and Frenchmen [*sic*] I am in no danger. People trust one another so much that they leave the gates and doors open."

In 1731, after fourteen years, the Mississippi Company gave up its charter. Financially the project had been a failure, perhaps the most appalling failure in the history of the New World, but it accomplished one very important thing for Louisiana, and that was to populate it, albeit willy-nilly, leaving it with 7,500 inhabitants instead of the 520 which it contained in 1717. The population of New Orleans itself in 1731 was nearly seven times what it had been ten years earlier, and the appearance of the city had greatly improved: contrast Father Charlevoix's description with that of Sister Madeleine Hachard de Saint-Stanislas in 1728: "Our town is very beautiful, well laid out and evenly built, as well as I can tell. The streets are wide and straight. The main street is a league long. The houses are well built of timber and mortar. Their tops are covered with shingles, which are little planks, sharpened in the form of slates—one must see them to believe it—for this roofing has all the appearance and beauty of slate. There is a popular song sung here which says that the city is as beautiful as Paris. Perhaps the song could convince people who have not seen the capital of France, but I have seen it, and the song does not persuade me to the contrary."

Sister Hachard and Father Charlevoix might have been speaking of two different cities, yet only seven years elapsed between the missionary's account and the nun's letter to her father—which, by the way, is one of the most delightful and informative documents of the Colonial period. "We have a farmyard and a garden," she wrote, "which adjoins a great woods of huge trees. From these woods come clouds of mosquitoes, gnats, and another kind of fly that I never met before and whose name—or surname—I do not know. At this moment several are sailing around me and wish to assassinate me. These wicked animals bite without mercy. We are assailed by them all night, but happily they go back to the woods in the day. . . . We drink beer, and our most ordinary food is rice with a little milk, little wild beans, meat and fish. In summer we eat little meat. It is killed but twice a week and it is difficult to keep in the heat. In the winter there is hunting, beginning in October, and ten miles from the town many wild animals are slaughtered and sold for three *sols* a pound— as is deer. Both are better than the beef and mutton we get in Rouen. Wild ducks are cheap and very common, but we buy scarcely any— we do not want to pamper ourselves. It is a charming country all winter and in summer there are the fish and oysters, fruits and sweet potatoes, which one cooks in the ashes, like chestnuts." But the pious sister could not resist speaking disapprovingly of the women in New Orleans, and there is perhaps also a touch of purely feminine envy in her description of their dress: "The women are careless of their salvation, but not of their vanity. Everyone here has luxuries, all of an equal magnificence. The greater part of them eat hominy but are dressed in velvet or damask, trimmed with ribbons. The women use powder and rouge to hide the wrinkles of their faces, and wear beauty-spots. The devil has a vast empire here, but that only strengthens our hope of destroying it, God willing."

[2]

One of the first actions of the Crown on resuming control of the colony was to reappoint Bienville as governor (Etienne de Périer had replaced him in 1726), and he served with distinction in this post for eleven more years, when at his own request he was recalled to France, where he spent the remaining twenty-five years of his life. In his place came a Canadian nobleman, Pierre Cavagnal de Rigaud, Marquis de Vaudreuil, son of the governor-general of Canada. Vaudreuil was a typical eighteenth century aristocrat—refined, courtly, and urbane —and his wife, the marquise, was a socially ambitious woman in whom the paradoxical vices of avarice and extravagance appear to have been blended in almost equal proportion. They entertained

PIERRE RIGAUD, MARQUIS DE VAUDREUIL,
GOVERNOR OF LOUISIANA 1743–1752

BATTLE OF NEW ORLEANS FROM A DRAWING BY AN EYEWITNESS

lavishly, and the little court of which they were the center came to acquire something of the jewel-like character of a *petit Versailles:* Vaudreuil himself was referred to as *le grand Marquis.* Generally they were well liked, and though there were occasional murmurs of favoritism and profiteering (two of the commonest charges against colonial administrators) it was with real reluctance that the colonists saw them leave in 1752 for Quebec, where Vaudreuil assumed the more important post, previously held by his father, of governor-general of Canada. During Vaudreuil's residence in New Orleans an incident occurred which deserves mentioning because it was the source of the first play written and produced in Louisiana. An Acolapissa Indian killed a Choctaw who he claimed had insulted his tribe; the murderer thereupon disappeared, and as the Choctaws were a powerful ally of the French, Vaudreuil was obliged to placate the relatives of the deceased. This could only be done by the blood sacrifice of an Acolapissa, and the murderer's father went to the Choctaws and allowed himself to be tomahawked in his son's place. A member of Vaudreuil's staff, a young officer named Leblanc de Villeneuve, who was an amateur poet and dramatist, wrote a verse play based on this occurrence; it was called *The Indian Father* and was performed at the governor's house. There is an interesting portrait of Vaudreuil by an anonymous contemporary artist which suggests a certain resemblance to Louis XV, but the Canadian's expression indicates much greater energy and intelligence.

His successor was Louis Billouard de Kerlérec, a French naval captain who immediately made himself unpopular with almost everyone (the Indians referred to him as Chef Menteur, or Chief Liar—a name, by the way, which survives in the local geography to designate the stream connecting Lake Pontchartrain to Lake Borgne and the Gulf). To do Kerlérec justice, however, the problems which confronted him during his administration were so numerous and of such a nature that they required almost superhuman strength and intelligence for their solution: there was constant fighting with the Chickasaws; there was the no less bitter, though bloodless, struggle for supremacy between the Capuchin and Jesuit orders (the Capuchins despised Kerlérec); and, worst of all, there were the British, with whom the French were at this time engaged in the all-out conflict known in this country as the French and Indian Wars: this, of course, was the prelude to the Seven Years' War, the first global conflict in history. As if these concerns were not enough, Kerlérec's assistant, a man named De Rochemore, was as difficult to get along with as was the governor himself; there was enmity between them from the first, and De Rochemore, who was both crafty and vindictive, at last succeeded in causing the removal of his superior: in June, 1763, Kerlérec was deported to France and imprisoned in the Bastille.

Meanwhile, in the court of Louis XV, there was growing dissatisfaction with the colony: Louisiana had proved unproductive commercially and was a source of constant expense. There was a certain prestige attached to owning it, but of this Louis XIV had been more conscious than his successor, whose ambitions, such as they were, certainly did not include empire building. Therefore, by an act passed at Fontainebleau on November 3, 1762, Louis XV offered to cede the entire colony to his cousin, Charles III of Spain (France and Spain were allies in the Seven Years' War). Charles III was no fool; he was almost certainly aware of his cousin's motives in wishing to rid himself of so troublesome a spot as Louisiana, as is evidenced by the fact that he was ten days in examining the mouth of this particular gift horse. Nevertheless he was tempted, and ended by accepting the offer: Louisiana became Spanish territory on September 13, 1762. The transaction was kept secret, and was not made known to the colonists until October, 1764, when it caused great consternation.

In the meantime, France and Spain had been defeated by the British in the Seven Years' War, and on November 3, 1762 (exactly two months after Louis XV had offered Louisiana to Spain and six and a half weeks after it had become Spanish property), the French and Spanish monarchs signed a treaty with the British king whereby the colony was split in half and all land east of the Mississippi, with the exception of the city of New Orleans, was given to Great Britain. New Orleans was assumed to remain French, though, as we have seen, it was really owned by Spain at the time. The local administrative posts continued to be held by Frenchmen—by Philippe d'Abbadie, who was appointed in 1763, and, at his death in 1765, by Philippe Aubry.

Shortly after Aubry's inauguration, a number of Acadian immigrants, refugees from Nova Scotia (whence they had been expelled by the British) began arriving in New Orleans: this is the migration described by Longfellow in *Evangeline*. Between January 1 and May 13, 1765, 650 of these refugees arrived in the city; they did not settle here, however, as they were mainly farmers, and went west across the river to the part of the state now sometimes referred to

as "French Louisiana"—more particularly, to Attakapas and Opelousas.

When D'Abbadie received a letter from the French prime minister,
the Duc de Choiseul, informing him that New Orleans had been under
Spanish rule for two years, and when he caused this information to be
proclaimed throughout the city, the popular reaction was one of
alarm, incredulity, and despair. The alliance between France and
Spain was a purely political one, based on a blood connection between
the two royal houses, and the French in Louisiana were suspicious of
the Spanish and fearful of domination by them. A petition was drawn
up, and Jean Milhet, the richest merchant in New Orleans, was se-
lected to go to Paris to plead with the prime minister that the city be
permitted to remain French. As soon as he arrived, he called on Bienville (then eighty-six years old) and the two went together to the
Duc de Choiseul. Gayarré says that Bienville, his voice shaken with
sobs, went down on his knees before the prime minister, but the latter
was firm in his refusal. Bienville never recovered from this disappoint-
ment, and died shortly thereafter.

Spain appointed as its first governor of Louisiana a distinguished
scientist, Don Antonio de Ulloa. Primarily an astronomer and mathe-
matician, an associate of Newton and Voltaire, he was also an inventor and jack of all scientific trades. In the nature and multiplicity
of his aptitudes he reminds one of his contemporary, Benjamin Franklin: he was interested, among other things, in electricity, in metal-
lurgy, in printing and engraving, and in natural history. Unlike
Franklin, however, he was no diplomat, and his unpopular position
as Spanish governor of a province which was French by culture and
popular sentiment called for diplomacy above everything else. He
did not arrive in New Orleans until March, 1766, nearly four years
after the transfer had been effected and eighteen months after news
of it had been made known in the colony, which was seething with
discontent. To make matters worse, he entered the city accompanied
by only ninety soldiers—a serious mistake on the part of the Spanish
government, which apparently underestimated the allegiance of the
colonists to the nation which had disowned them. This was an open
invitation to rebellion, though it was generally assumed that more
Spanish troops were on their way, and Ulloa further antagonized the
citizens when he refused to lay his credentials before the Superior
Council, saying that Aubry was the only authority with whom he
would have any dealings.

The Superior Council was headed by an attorney, Nicolas Chauvin de Lafrénière, who was the most articulate spokesman in Louisiana for French domination. Historians—even the Louisiana historians of French descent—are divided in their attitudes toward Lafrénière: Gayarré plainly regards him as a troublemaker, while Fortier considers him a patriot of the highest order. Though aware of the failure of Milhet's mission to Paris, he and many other colonists continued to believe, even after the arrival of Ulloa, that the Spanish transfer might be revoked. "It seems," writes Gayarré, "as if nothing could convince the colonists that the cession of Louisiana to Spain was serious and conclusive." For over two and a half years Ulloa remained in Louisiana as nominal governor, though the administration of the colony, for all practical purposes, remained in the hands of Aubry and the Superior Council. The Spaniard spent most of his time at the mouth of the Mississippi, making observations on the local flora and fauna and immersed in scientific studies. When he finally returned to New Orleans, the citizens neglected no opportunity to make him and his wife, the former Marchioness of Abrado, feel unwanted. There were many charges against them, at least one of which does them credit: Ulloa had forbidden slaves to be whipped in New Orleans because their cries upset his wife, and the natives complained of the inconvenience of having to take their Negroes six miles outside the city limits in order to punish them. Ulloa and his high-born wife must have been acutely miserable during their residence in New Orleans. A letter from Kerlérec, now languishing in the Bastille, did not improve the governor's spirits: "From the bottom of my heart I pity you for having been sent to such a country."

At last the feeling of the people, worked upon by Lafrénière and emboldened by the failure of the long-expected Spanish troops to arrive, exploded: a petition was drawn up calling for the expulsion of Ulloa. On October 29, 1768, the Superior Council approved the petition and, ignoring the objections of Aubry, who remained loyal to Ulloa, issued a decree ordering the governor to leave the colony in three days' time; its members justified their action mainly on the technical ground that Ulloa had never formally presented them with his credentials. The decree was delivered to the governor on board a Spanish frigate in the river, to which he had, on the advice of Aubry, taken refuge, and on November 1st he sailed for Havana, where he wrote a detailed report to the home government in which he named the leaders of the revolt and described the part that each of them had played therein.

Aubry's position had been even more awkward than Ulloa's. Of French blood himself, and loyal to the French Crown, he nevertheless recognized the legality of the cession and acknowledged Ulloa as rightful governor, although to do so meant forfeiting the friendship of nearly every influential citizen in New Orleans and incurring the enmity of the Superior Council. A revolution against Spain, he reasoned, would constitute an offense to both Crowns, and from the first he tried to dissuade Lafrénière and the Superior Council from taking so radical a step. "Remember," he said finally, "that the chiefs of a conspiracy have always met with a tragical end."

The peculiar difficulty of Aubry's situation may be inferred from his dispatches at this time to the French government: "I am in one of the most extraordinary positions," he wrote in January, 1768. "I command for the king of France, and, at the same time, I govern the colony as if it belonged to the king of Spain. . . . It is no pleasant mission to govern a colony which undergoes so many revolutions, which has not known, for three years, whether it was Spanish or French." After Ulloa's expulsion, he wrote: "I was waiting only for the arrival of the Spanish troops, to deliver up the colony, and to return to France to render an account of my conduct, when a general rebellion of the inhabitants of this province against the Spanish Governor and his nation, which it was not in my power to oppose, and which occurred on the 28th and 29th of October, destroyed in a moment the work of four years, and all the dispositions which I had taken on behalf of the crown of Spain. An audacious petition, insulting to the Spanish nation, rebellious against the king of France, was presented to demand Ulloa's expulsion."

When Ulloa's report of the revolution reached Madrid, it caused considerable consternation. A cabinet council of six grandees was formed to consider the problem, and it is interesting to note that one of these, Don Miguel de Muzquiz, recommended returning Louisiana to France. From a letter of the Marquis of Grimaldi to the Spanish ambassador at Versailles, we know that Charles III was much upset when he learned of the revolt: what he chiefly resented was the blow to his pride. Following Ulloa's departure, the colonists had drawn up a manifesto justifying their action, and copies of this document, to the intense annoyance of the Spanish monarch, had found their way into the columns of several European journals under the caption "Paris News."

Spain, as if to compensate for her previous neglect, now acted quickly and decisively. On July 24, 1769, word reached New Orleans that a fleet of twenty-four Spanish vessels had arrived at the mouth of the river and was preparing to proceed upstream; the number of men on board was three thousand, which was almost the equivalent of the entire population of New Orleans. As commander of this expedition Charles III had sent Don Alexander O'Reilly, an Irish soldier of fortune in the service of Spain; he had once saved the king's life in a riot and had been ennobled for this and other services. On August 15th, at an impressive ceremony in the Place d'Armes, O'Reilly took formal possession of the colony in the name of Charles III. The twelve leaders of the revolution were arrested and tried: five of them, including Lafrénière and a nephew of Bienville, were sentenced to death, and six others, including Jean Milhet, received prison sentences. Joseph Villeré (whose descendants are living in the city today) died while awaiting trial, and a thirteenth conspirator, the Intendant Commissary Foucault, was later arrested and deported to France, where he was placed in the Bastille. The execution took place on October 25th, at the corner of what is now Barracks and Decatur streets, and the feelings of the citizens may be inferred from the fact that although a large fee was offered for a hangman no white man in the city could be found for the purpose. O'Reilly, who felt it would be unwise, considering the public state of mind, to permit five of the city's leading citizens to meet their death at the hands of a Negro, consented finally to a firing squad: Spain thus avenged her honor, and, seven years before the signing of the Declaration of Independence, stamped out the first revolt of a European colony in the New World.

In his capacity as avenging military governor, O'Reilly reorganized the colony as a dependency of Cuba. Although a few French laws— including the *Code Noir*—were retained, the "wise and pious laws of Spain" (to quote O'Reilly) were instituted generally and continued in effect during the whole of the Spanish domination with the exception of one which proved so unpopular that it was repealed; it provided "that the married woman who commits adultery, and her companion, be delivered to the husband for him to do with what he pleases, provided that he cannot kill the one without killing the other." O'Reilly abolished the Superior Council, substituting a Cabildo, or municipal governing body similar to those in other Spanish colonies. Spanish became the official tongue, but French continued to be spoken by the majority of citizens.

His task accomplished, O'Reilly installed Don Luís de Unzaga of Ameragua as third Spanish governor of Louisiana, and left New Orleans in October, 1770. Unzaga was both mild and efficient, and under his kindly administration the colonists began gradually to be reconciled to Spanish rule. The common enemy of France and Spain in America was, of course, Great Britain, and this was another circumstance which made for cooperation on the part of the colonists. A third power, destined to check British imperialism forever south of the Canadian border, was in process of formation—the thirteen original colonies on the Atlantic seaboard, and the extent to which Spain supported the new nation, while remaining technically neutral, is not generally realized. Unzaga (who was worried lest England should extend her empire beyond the Mississippi) supplied the Americans with secret gifts of arms; so did his successor, the gallant Bernardo de Galvez, who also, when Spain finally declared war, wrested Baton Rouge from the British and conducted successful sieges against Mobile and Pensacola, expelling the enemy from the Gulf of Mexico. Unzaga further pleased the New Orleanians by marrying one of them, a Mademoiselle St. Maxent, thus setting an official example for the mingling of French and Spanish strains in the city, and Galvez did likewise. The capture of Baton Rouge, which the British had renamed New Richmond, inspired a New Orleans merchant, Julien Poydras (after whom an important street is named) to write an epic poem dealing with the career of Galvez: it was published in 1779, and, if we except Villeneuve's play, is the first contribution in French to the local literature.

A vivid description of life in the colony in 1776 occurs in a memoir of Don Francisco de Bouligny, an officer in Galvez' army. "The inhabitants of this country," he wrote, "may be divided into three classes: planters, merchants, and day-laborers. . . . The greater number of planters who live in the vicinity of New Orleans are the most refined people in this country. Many of them were officers during the French domination, and some are decorated with the Cross of Saint Louis. . . . The second class—the merchants—are occupied only in buying and selling and in making occasional journeys to distant posts, eager to be able to earn enough to become planters. . . . The third class work two or three days in the week, and spend the remainder of their time in the taverns." Speaking of the plantation houses, he noted: "The houses are convenient, according to the climate; all have a very wide gallery or covered balcony, which surrounds them, for protection against the intense heat of the summer, and there are fire-places in all the rooms for the winter, which sometimes is severe. All the houses are thirty or forty feet from the bank of the river, because they are pleasanter thus, and it is easier to embark and debark, as everything is conducted by water. The houses are of wood, brick, and mortar, and the kitchen is about twenty paces to the rear of the house. There is a garden or orchard, especially in the country." The Negroes, he observed, "are slaves in name only, for in reality they are as happy as may be the laborers in Europe. The master is obliged only to give each Negro a barrel of corn, and a piece of ground for him to grow his crop of corn, rice, or whatever he may wish, a cabin, a yard of thirty or forty paces with a fence, for him to raise chickens, hogs, etc. With his profits, each Negro buys every winter a woolen coat, a pair of long breeches, and two or three shirts. With what remains to him he buys bear's grease, to cook, as he pleases, the corn on which they all live and are so healthy and robust that some persons who came here lately from Havana were astonished to see the Negroes so nimble, strong, and bright." Noting the absence of beggars ("One does not see a single beggar in the whole province"), Bouligny added: "Some mariners who have come from Havana, accustomed to ask for alms, more through habit than through necessity, wished to do the same; but as all the women went to the doors of their houses at this novelty, and told them the same thing—that it was a shame that men, young and strong, should be so lazy—they were obliged to return to their vessel, giving up the idea of drawing a profit from that industry."

Two disastrous events—appalling at the time but destined to prove blessings in disguise, since they were to cause great improvements in the appearance of the city—occurred during the administrations of Don Estevan Miró and Don Francisco Luís Hector, Baron de Caron-delet: they were the fires of 1788 and 1794. The first of these occurred on Good Friday. Starting in the house of a public official at Chartres and Toulouse streets, it laid waste most of the houses (which were built of wood) in the city with the exception of those fronting on the water; as there was a strong breeze from the river, these were spared. In all, 856 buildings were destroyed, among them the cathedral and the Town Hall. There is a story—perhaps apocry-phal—that, it being Good Friday, the priests would not allow the church bells to be used as a fire alarm, and that this circumstance was responsible for the extent of the destruction. New Orleans had hardly been rebuilt before it was ravaged by a second fire, which, originating in the back yard of a house on Royal Street, got quickly out of hand and burned 212 buildings. One third of the houses in the city—and those among the newest and the best—were demolished, and, though fewer buildings were involved than in the previous conflagration, the financial loss was believed to be heavier. Fortunately the cathedral, which had just been finished, was spared. As protection against future fires, the authorities offered premiums to those citizens who, in re-building their houses, used tiles instead of shingles on their roofs. Most of the oldest houses in the city today therefore date from the Spanish domination, as only a very few survived both of these disas-ters: the new structures were of brick, covered with stucco; they were built about a patio in the Spanish manner and featured bal-conies with iron grilles, exactly as in Andalusia and the colonies in Mexico and Cuba. The public buildings, largely through the philan-thropy of Don Andrés Almonaster y Roxas, a rich citizen who paid for the new cathedral as well as for the Cabildo to its right, were quickly replaced and were vastly superior to the old ones.

When news of the French Revolution reached New Orleans, there was much excitement. Spain, shocked by the execution (on January 2, 1793) of Louis XVI, promptly declared war on the new govern-ment, and the situation in New Orleans became critical. Loyalties were divided three ways: toward Spain, toward the old monarchy, and toward the Republicans. The last of these was the most common, as the colonists had never quite forgiven Louis XV for handing them over to Spain. Revolutionary songs were sung in the theaters, in the taverns, and in the streets. Some of the colonists, heedless of La-frénière's tragic example, even went so far as to petition the new gov-ernment to be placed under its protection. The Spanish governor, Baron de Carondelet, proved equal to the emergency. Acting with admirable tact and efficiency, he immediately prohibited all public gatherings and popular demonstrations of sympathy with the Re-public, and jailed a few of the more overt agitators. In this way he disposed of a situation which could very easily have exploded and caused untold bloodshed, for Spain would not lightly have accepted another such blow to her pride.

In New Orleans, the French Revolution produced one culturally significant event: following the successful slave uprising (which was an offshoot of the Revolution) in Santo Domingo, a number of refugees came to the city, among whom was a company of actors from Cap Français. In 1792 they opened a theater on St. Peter Street, where they presented the first professional performances in Louisiana. Two years later, the colony's first regular newspaper, the *Moniteur de la Louisiane*, made its appearance, published in French; its files are now indispensable to any serious student of the local history. Still a third event occurred during the Spanish domination which was to revitalize Louisiana's agricultural economy—the dramatic discovery, in 1795, by Etienne de Boré, who owned a plantation six miles above the city, of the granulation process for manufacturing sugar. New Orleans was also much excited by the visit, in 1798, of three exiled nobles: the Duke of Orléans, a direct descendant (great-great-grandson) of the regent after whom the city was named, and his two brothers, the Duke of Montpensier and the Count of Beaujolais. They were entertained magnificently at the homes of Pierre de Marigny, Julien Poydras, and Etienne de Boré, whose invention had made him rich as well as famous. Marigny made a cash loan to the Duke of Orléans, and when the latter became King Louis Philippe of France, thirty-two years later, he repaid Pierre's son, Bernard, with costly presents and educated him in France at the royal expense.

Meanwhile, in Europe, events were occurring which were to change once more the status of Louisiana. Another empire builder, Napoleon Bonaparte, had become master of France and was casting covetous eyes on the colony. In 1800, Joseph de Pontalba, a Creole who had been educated in France and who had become a colonel in the *Grande Armée*, presented to Napoleon a report which he had drawn up describing the condition of Louisiana in minute detail. After pointing out the wealth of its natural resources, he added: "The inhabitant of Louisiana . . . would give half of his blood to be replaced under French domination, and would shed the last drop of the remaining half to defend that domination." Napoleon was not long in making up his mind: Pontalba's report was submitted to him on September 15th, and only fifteen days later he signed with Spain the Treaty of San Ildefonso, according to which, in return for certain concessions, Louisiana was once more to become the property of France. This cession, like the earlier one, was kept secret, as Napoleon feared that the British would attack the colony if they knew it had passed into French hands. Three years later, when hostilities were suspended temporarily by the Peace of Amiens, he commissioned

Pierre de Laussat to go to Louisiana with the title of Colonial Prefect. Laussat arrived in New Orleans on March 21, 1803, but did not immediately take formal possession of the colony, awaiting the arrival from Santo Domingo of Napoleon's brother-in-law, General Charles Victor Emanuel Leclerc, who was to be chief administrator.

[3]

But Napoleon was not the only one to covet Louisiana. When President Thomas Jefferson heard by way of the grapevine that Spain had secretly ceded the colony to France, that astute statesman had been seriously alarmed. To Europeans, Napoleon had proved a difficult neighbor: what would it be like to have him at the mouth of the Mississippi? Jefferson instructed Secretary of State James Madison to have the American minister in Paris, Robert R. Livingston, investigate the rumor, and when Livingston confirmed it Jefferson immediately ordered him to negotiate with Napoleon for purchase of New Orleans; this was the part of Louisiana in which Jefferson was chiefly interested, for he wanted the navigation rights of the river and the use of its principal port. The matter of the cession was hotly debated in the American Congress even before Laussat's arrival—while he was en route, in fact—and some members advocated extreme and violent methods. Senator James Ross, of Pennsylvania, asked, "Why not seize, then, what is so essential to us as a nation? Why not expel the wrong-doers?" and Senator James Jackson, of Georgia, expressed himself as follows: "Bonaparte, in our Southern country, would be lost, with all his martial talents. . . . With a body of only 10,000 of our expert riflemen around him, his laurels would be torn from his brow, and he would heartily wish himself once more on the plains of Italy." Jefferson himself declared: "By taking this port, France has committed an act of hostility. She forces us to ally ourselves with the English fleet and nation."

Finally Jefferson appointed his friend James Monroe as Envoy Extraordinary to France in order to help Livingston intercede with Napoleon to part with New Orleans for a price. As it turned out, he could not possibly have chosen a more appropriate time, for Napoleon was on the eve of renewing the war with England, and he realized that he would lose Louisiana to the British if he did not sell it to the United States. The Marquis of Barbé-Marbois, who was Treasurer of

France at the time and who wrote an interesting *History of Louisiana*, says that Napoleon summoned him on Easter Sunday, April 10, 1803, and told him: "I know all the value of Louisiana, and I have wished to repair the error of the French negotiator who abandoned it in 1763. A few lines of a treaty have given it back to me, and hardly have I recovered it when I must expect to lose it. But if I lose it, it will be dearer one day to those who compel me to abandon it than to those to whom I wish to deliver it. The English have successively taken away from France: Canada, Cape Breton, Newfoundland, Acadia, the richest parts of Asia. They shall not have the Mississippi, which they covet. . . . The conquest of Louisiana would be easy if they merely took the trouble to land there. I have not a moment to lose if I wish to place it out of their reach." When Marbois observed that the colonists themselves would almost certainly object to being sold once more in this fashion, Napoleon replied: "That is, indeed, in all its perfection the ideology of the right of nature and of nations. But I must have money to make war against the nation that has the most money. Send your doctrine to London; I am sure it will be the subject of great admiration, and yet no great attention is paid to it when it is a question of taking possession of the finest countries in Asia." He added prophetically: "Perhaps, also, it will be objected that the Americans may be found too powerful for Europe in two or three centuries, but my foresight does not embrace these remote fears. Besides, one may expect in the future rivalries within the Union itself." When Napoleon made this remark, the man who was to fire the opening shot of the Civil War was already fifteen years old: Pierre Gustave Toutant Beauregard, a Louisianian.

The following morning, in another audience, Napoleon told Marbois: "I renounce Louisiana. It is not only New Orleans that I wish to cede; it is the whole colony, without reserving any part of it. I know the value of what I abandon, and I have proved sufficiently the importance that I attach to that province since my first diplomatic act with Spain was for the object of its recovery. I renounce it, therefore, with great regret. To insist upon its preservation would be madness. I direct you to negotiate this affair with envoys of Congress. Do not even wait for the arrival of Mr. Monroe; have an interview this very day with Mr. Livingston." On the same day, Livingston wrote to Madison: "M. Talleyrand asked me this day, when pressing the subject, whether we wished to have the whole of Louisiana. I told him no. . . . He said that if they gave New Orleans the rest would be of little value, and that he would wish to know 'what we would give for the whole.' " Livingston offered twenty million francs on the spot; this was rejected, and after further negotiation a cash price of sixty million francs, roughly twelve million dollars, was agreed upon. It must be remembered that the province of Louisiana at this time included the entire area west of the Mississippi as far as the Rocky Mountains: thus Jefferson paid something like four cents an acre for land whose potential wealth was incalculable. The American cession was signed in Paris on April 30th, five weeks after Laussat had arrived in New Orleans and before he had formally taken possession of the colony. He had, to be sure, shortly after his arrival issued a proclamation announcing that Louisiana once more belonged to France, and though some citizens were uneasy over the news (fearing under Republican rule a slave revolution such as had occurred in Santo Domingo) the majority of them were pleased, and a group of planters wrote to Laussat saying, "The old men repeat on all sides: 'We may die now, we are French.' "

When, in the summer of 1803, Laussat heard a rumor that Napoleon had sold the colony to the United States, he was incredulous, terming it an "impudent and incredible falsehood." But soon he received official confirmation of it; a vessel arrived from Bordeaux with the news that, on June 6th, Napoleon had authorized him commissioner to take possession of the colony in the name of France and afterwards to deliver it to the United States. At a ceremony in the Cabildo, the Spanish governor, Don Manuel de Salcedo, and his assistant, Don Carlos de la Puerta y O'Farrell, Marquis de Casa Calvo, handed him the keys of the city, and Spanish rule in Louisiana came to a formal end. It had lasted some thirty-five years and had, on the whole, been beneficial to the colony. The population of New Orleans had more than trebled: in 1803 there were ten thousand inhabitants, nearly half of whom were Negroes. The city had been completely rebuilt with handsome and permanent structures, and under the administration of the Spanish governors public morale was generally higher than it had ever been under French rule, as the citizens themselves finally came to realize. A delegation of planters, in welcoming Laussat, declared: "We have no cause of complaint against the Spanish government. We have never groaned under the iron yoke of an offensive despotism." In another welcome ceremony he was told by a group of New Orleanians: "Perhaps France would attach less value to the homage of our fidelity if she saw us relinquishing without any regret our allegiance to the sovereign who has loaded us with favors, during all the time he has reigned over us. Such culpable indifference is not to be found in our hearts, in which our regret at separating from him occupies as much space as our joy in securing the nationality we had lost." A propos of these appreciations of Spain, Gayarré comments: "These two addresses are very remarkable testimonials in favor of the Spanish administration in Louisiana. It is not often that departing power is greeted with such hosannas, and that the incense of public worship is offered to the setting sun."

On the same day that Laussat received the city in the name of the French Republic, he issued a proclamation informing the bewildered citizens that they were soon to become Americans. He abolished the Cabildo, installed Etienne de Boré as first mayor of New Orleans, and awaited the arrival of the American commissioners, General James Wilkinson and William C. C. Claiborne, governor of the Mississippi Territory. Twenty days later, at another ceremony on the same spot, the French flag was lowered and the American flag raised in its place. The newcomers began arriving almost immediately—hordes of them, from Ohio, Illinois, Kentucky, even from east of the Alleghenies. Some came to settle, some merely to trade. Because it was both river port and seaport, New Orleans was an ideal agricultural market for the entire Middle West: as Jefferson observed, "There is no spot on the globe to which the produce of so great an extent of fertile country must necessarily come."

The steamboat had not yet been invented, and the traders loaded their merchandise on flatboats, keelboats, and all manner of primitive and sometimes fantastic-looking vessels which were floated down the river and hauled upstream in various ways—by poling, by means of ropes fastened to trees along the shore and pulled by the crew (bush-whacking), or by ropes fastened to the vessel's mast and pulled by a team of longshoremen. It has been estimated that between 1803 and 1830 more than a thousand such boats made the trip to New Orleans annually; there was a huge flatboat harbor at Tchoupitoulas Street. The flatboat men were among the toughest to be found anywhere—a brawling, roistering lot who, when they reached the city, squandered their pay in the taverns, brothels, and gambling dens which quickly sprang up along the Tchoupitoulas Street riverfront and in the still more disreputable quarter known as the Swamp, ten blocks away from the river on Girod Street. For thirty-five or forty years—until the advent of the steamboat and for nearly a decade afterward—

the flatboat and keelboat men were colorful and familiar figures in the streets of New Orleans; in spite of the business which they brought, however, they were dreaded by the majority of the law-abiding citizens—particularly by the Creoles, with whom they were especially inclined to pick fights. It was the river men, incidentally, who first coined the term "Dixie" to mean New Orleans: the word was not used to apply to the South as a whole until the Civil War; it is a corruption, or rather a mispronunciation, of the French *dix*, which was printed on ten-dollar notes issued by one of the city banks.

As a result of the river traffic, New Orleans began to mushroom. Merchants, investors, and speculators came from all over the country, and as there was no room for them in the French Quarter, they settled across Canal Street in the suburb known as the Faubourg Ste. Marie. There were thus two rival cities, representing civilizations which were poles apart. It must be remembered that the Creoles were Americans only by an act of Congress; eleven more years were to pass before they were to feel themselves a part of the Union—when, under Andrew Jackson, they were to fight side by side with the Americans against a common enemy, the British. "I have discovered with regret," wrote Claiborne to James Madison, "that a strong partiality for the French Government still exists among many of the inhabitants of this City." The Creoles were resentful of the newcomers, whom they regarded as usurpers. Their experience with the riverboat men had embittered them against Americans generally, and they made no distinction between the riffraff of which this class was composed and the respectable businessmen who began arriving in their wake: they designated all of them by the contemptuous term "Kaintuck." The word became synonymous in Creole society with barbarian—a household article with which to threaten unruly children. In certain haughty old Creole families this prejudice lasted for generations, surviving both the War of 1812 and the Civil War, and intermarriage with *les Américains* was frowned on right up to the beginning of the present century.

It is true that the Creoles were culturally superior to the Americans at this time. Among the latter there were a few families of refinement and education, but they were vastly outnumbered by a rabble of whom the best that can be said is that they were not lacking in energy and were frequently ambitious. There were no immigration restrictions, and a large criminal element was attracted, with the result that as early as 1805 there existed in New Orleans a genuine underworld

which derived its income from the vices of the river men. Policing
the city became a problem of major proportions from the earliest
years of the American occupation, and of the two elements the
Creoles were by far the more law-abiding. They were destined to
be outnumbered shortly by the Americans, however, for the latter
continued to arrive in large numbers and there was only one significant addition to the French-speaking population after 1803: this was
when a group of refugees from the slave revolution in Santo Domingo
who had settled in Cuba were obliged to relocate because of anti-
French feeling there caused by Napoleon's invasion of Spain. New
Orleans was the logical place for them to come, and between 1805
and 1810 as many as 8,000 arrived in the city; the biggest wave occurred in the spring of 1809, when thirty-four vessels containing
5,500 immigrants docked at the city's wharves, causing a shortage in
housing and food supplies. Only a third of this number were whites;
the remainder were free *gens de couleur* and slaves. It was these West
Indian slaves, incidentally, who introduced the Voodoo cult into
Louisiana.

Louisiana was not made a state immediately. It was divided into
two parts; the northern, called the District of Louisiana, was to be
under the administration of the governor of the Indiana Territory,
and the remainder (including most of the present state) was organized
independently as the Territory of Orleans, with Claiborne as governor. The question as to whether Louisianians were capable of self-
government had been debated in Washington with considerable spirit,
and Claiborne himself was dubious of their fitness in this respect.
Within the Territory, an effort was made to replace the old French
and Spanish laws with the Common Law of England. This caused
considerable confusion, for the latter was unwritten, and the concept
of unwritten law was unfamiliar to the Latin mind: what finally
emerged was a system based largely on the *Code Napoléon*, and com-
bining features of both the Common Law and the Roman Law.
Louisiana law is still very different from that of other states: to this
day, because of the Napoleonic Code, the Federal Government cannot levy inheritance taxes on a widow or a widower.

Claiborne's administration was a troubled one, marked by a number
of unsettling events: by Spanish incursions on the western boundary
of the Territory; by the conspiracy of Aaron Burr, who sought to
establish an empire in the Southwest; and by the activities of pirates
in Barataria Bay under the leadership of Jean Lafitte. The boundary

of West Florida, which still belonged to Spain, had never been satisfactorily settled; neither had the boundary between the Orleans Territory and Texas (also a Spanish possession) on the west. Spain was marshaling forces on the Texas frontier, and in September, 1806, Jefferson dispatched General Wilkinson to prevent any encroachments on what he regarded as American soil. The rival forces camped on opposite sides of the Sabine River, and the Spanish made no attempt to penetrate beyond this point.

While Wilkinson was engaged in these maneuvers, he received a secret message from Aaron Burr, soliciting his aid in a conspiracy the purpose of which was to create a separate empire of the Territory of Orleans. Burr was an extraordinary figure. He had been elected Vice President of the United States in 1801, after nearly defeating Jefferson for the Presidency, and had killed Alexander Hamilton in a duel three years later. He was an intimate friend of Andrew Jackson, and had interested a number of prominent persons, among them Wilkinson himself, in his scheme for seizing the Orleans Territory. Confronted with a choice, Wilkinson hesitated for several days, and finally made it: he wrote to Jefferson on October 8, 1806, informing him that a conspiracy was afoot. He did not name Burr specifically in his letter, but it was not really necessary for him to do so, as Burr's plans were by this time an open secret, particularly in Kentucky and the Middle West, where he had his largest following; Jefferson had already appointed a secret agent, a man named Graham, who was Secretary of the Treasury, to report on his movements. Burr had twice previously been brought to trial for treason, but Henry Clay, his attorney, had won him acquittals. Jefferson once more ordered his arrest, and on January 17, 1806, he was seized in the Mississippi Territory while en route to New Orleans, was released on bail, and fled to Alabama, where he was again arrested, and taken to Richmond, Virginia. Miraculously, he was acquitted yet a third time in a sensational trial which attracted international interest.

The Barataria pirates posed an even more difficult problem for Governor Claiborne. Ever since the eighteenth century Barataria Bay and the labyrinth of bayous which flowed into it some sixty miles southwest of New Orleans had been a hideout for pirates. Bluebeard himself, shortly before he met his death off the Carolina coast in 1718, is supposed to have taken refuge there. They continued to infest the coast area right on down into the nineteenth century, and when the Louisiana Purchase opened up the Mississippi River to traders from the West and Middle West, New Orleans became the principal market for pirates to dispose of their plunder. Naturally, this merchandise could not be cleared through the customs; it had to be smuggled into the city, and bases were established on the islands of Grande Terre and Grand Isle, at the entrance to Barataria Bay, where contraband material could be stored pending sale to New Orleans merchants, who visited the islands surreptitiously. Between 1805 and 1813, Grande Terre and Grand Isle became built up with saloons, bordellos, and gambling dens (gambling is still a problem at Grand Isle) and was attracting as vicious a band of cutthroats as ever assembled in the New World. Properly speaking, however, they were not really a band, for there was no organization: the men were forever brawling among themselves, no one's life or property was safe, and the place finally became so dangerous that merchants were afraid to visit it, with the result that the pirates' business suffered seriously.

The man who was to become the leader of the Barataria pirates, and to organize them so that they could function with profit and efficiency, was a Frenchman named Jean Lafitte, who had come to Louisiana with his brother, Pierre, in 1806. For a while the pair operated a store on Royal Street where they dealt in smuggled goods; there is a legend that they also owned a blacksmith shop on the corner of Bourbon and St. Philip streets, but it has never been authenticated. When the slave trade was abolished in 1808, the price of slaves soared so high that smuggling them into the country became an enormously lucrative activity, and Jean Lafitte decided to enter it. Leaving his brother in charge of the store, he went to Grande Terre, the larger of the two settlements. The pirates who enjoyed the greatest prestige on the island were Dominique You, a former artilleryman in Napoleon's army; Vincent Gambi, a particularly villainous Italian with a long criminal history; and "Cut Nose" Chinghizola, so called because of a facial disfigurement incurred in a saber fight. (Descendants of Chinghizola are living today on Grand Isle, and there is a street there bearing their name.) Lafitte gained their intimacy and proposed a plan, to which they listened with interest, for reorganizing the colony. It has been said that in a week's time he acquired command over all the Barataria pirates; this is probably an exaggeration, but it cannot be denied that he possessed unusual capacity for organization and leadership, and in a short time came to be acknowledged as the ruler and master mind of Barataria. He built a luxurious mansion on Grande Terre where he entertained important visitors from New Orleans, among them John Grimes, the local district attorney. Under his leadership the colony prospered to such an extent that it represented a serious threat to legitimate business in New Orleans, and Governor Claiborne was alarmed. He offered a reward of $500 to anyone who would deliver Lafitte to him, and the pirate retaliated by offering $1,500 to anyone who would bring the governor to Grande Terre—an anecdote, and a true one, which is familiar to every Louisiana schoolboy. Claiborne was at his wits' end. In 1814 he arrested and imprisoned Jean's brother, Pierre, charging him with collusion, but Pierre, probably by bribing the prison officials, somehow managed to escape, and joined his brother at Grande Terre.

Meanwhile the British, with whom this country was engaged in the War of 1812 and who had just burned the Capitol in Washington, were preparing to attack New Orleans. In the fall of 1814, an English brig entered Barataria Bay under the command of Captain Nicholas Lockyer, who sought and obtained an interview with Lafitte: the purpose of this visit was to solicit the pirates' aid in attacking the city, in return for which Lafitte was offered a sizable sum of money and a captainship in the Royal Navy. Lockyer further made it clear that, should he refuse, all the Barataria pirates would be exterminated in the event of a British victory. Lafitte asked for time in which to think the matter over. He and his lieutenants were under grand-jury indictments for piracy, and the idea occurred to him that if he were to offer his services to the Federal Government at this important juncture, the indictments might be quashed and he and his men given United States citizenship. He therefore wrote at once to the authorities in New Orleans, informing them of the impending invasion and assuring them of his loyalty. "Though proscribed by my adoptive country," he began his letter, "I will never let slip any occasion of serving her or of proving that she has never ceased to be dear to me." His offer, however, was ignored: Claiborne had referred it to General Andrew Jackson, then in Mobile, and Jackson (whose phrase for Lafitte's men was "hellish banditti") had turned it down.

When it became apparent from other sources that the British planned to attack Louisiana, President James Madison ordered Jackson to New Orleans. It was high time: three days later, a British fleet of fifty vessels sailed from Jamaica bound for Lake Borgne, which could be entered from the Gulf of Mexico; the British planned to attack from the northeast shore of this lake. The importance which England attached to this expedition can be inferred from the fact that its command had been offered to the Duke of Wellington, whose prestige (after Waterloo) was practically unlimited; Wellington, however, sent his brother-in-law, Sir Edward Pakenham, in his place. Gayarré estimates the invading army at 14,450 men, which is perhaps an exaggeration. At any rate, it included veterans of many a European campaign, some of whom had helped to hold Napoleon back at Waterloo.

The British arrived at Lake Borgne on December 14th, and in an engagement off Malheureux Island easily defeated the puny force of 180 men which had gathered to resist them. In this engagement they lost three hundred of the twelve hundred men they sent ashore (among them was Lieutenant Pratt, who had set fire to the Capitol), and the Americans lost sixty—a loss which they could ill afford, considering the extent to which they were outnumbered—and were obliged to retreat, leaving the enemy in control of the lake.

New Orleans was now in a fever of alarm. She was practically defenseless, as the five gunboats with which the Federal Government had supplied her had all been captured in the Battle of Lake Borgne, and had the British pressed forward at this point there is little doubt that they could have captured the city. They hesitated, however, thinking her better defended than she was, and this delay enabled Jackson to prepare for their coming. He declared martial law in New Orleans, requiring every able-bodied citizen to take up arms, and wrote to General Coffee in Baton Rouge and to other generals in the Southern area for reinforcements. Once more Lafitte renewed his offer: heedless of the fine on his head, he went to Jackson this time in person, and the latter, who needed every man he could get, decided to accept his assistance. The British had prepared their attack carefully: aware of the antipathy which many Creoles still felt toward the Americans, they had printed circulars in French and Spanish which they caused to be distributed surreptitiously: "Louisianians! Remain quiet in your houses; your slaves shall be preserved to you, and your property respected. We make war only against Americans." On December 22nd they advanced as far as the Villeré plantation, only eight miles from the city, and Jackson, whose forces had been augmented by a brigade of mounted riflemen from Tennessee under General Coffee and a detachment of Tennessee militia commanded by Major General Carroll, rode out to meet them. In the skirmish which followed, the British lost about three hundred men and the Americans a third of that number. The enemy advance was checked temporarily, but they were massing their troops for a final decisive battle, and Jackson knew it. He established his position along the Rodríguez Canal, a ditch running from the river to the swamps, a distance of about half a mile, and along the bank of this ditch he threw up a primitive breastwork of wooden fenceposts strengthened with cotton bales. On the other side of the ditch lay the plain of Chalmette, which was to be the battlefield. Jackson's total forces by this time numbered a little under four thousand men. In addition to Louisianians (among whom was an outfit of free men of color, Choctaw Indians, and Barataria pirates) there were General Coffee's and General Carroll's Tennesseeans, some volunteer dragoons from the Mississippi Territory, and 2,250 Kentucky militiamen who arrived at the very last minute. The Americans were also supported from the river by two naval vessels, the *Carolina* and the *Louisiana*.

Early on the morning of January 8th, Pakenham's scarlet-coated men advanced in neat, orderly formations which were quickly thinned by volleys from the American line. Again and again they approached (some even gained the breastwork, and were killed in attempting to mount it), but Jackson's men drove them back repeatedly. The fiercest part of the battle raged between dawn and eight-thirty: by two in the afternoon the British had retreated for good, leaving behind them on the battlefield more than two thousand dead and wounded. Major Latour, one of Jackson's officers, says that a space of ground 200 by 250 yards "was literally covered with men, either dead or severely wounded." Among the former were Pakenham and other high-ranking British officers.

It was a great triumph for Jackson. Only seven of his men had been killed, and six wounded. Wellington's veterans had been no match for the sharpshooters from the backwoods country, and yet it cannot be said that they displayed anything but the greatest gallantry. The Battle of New Orleans must rank as one of the most phenomenal in military history. "It was an application," writes W. Adolphe Roberts in his book on Lake Pontchartrain, "of the formal methods of European warfare on a terrain where these were an absurdity, and against men whose *forte* was a deadly marksmanship."

Needless to say, there was much rejoicing in the city. Jackson was honored at an impressive ceremony in the Place d'Armes, the square which was later to bear his name, and at a *Te Deum* service in the cathedral. None of Old Hickory's military exploits earned him greater renown than the defense of New Orleans, and it was not forgotten when, fourteen years later, he campaigned successfully for the Presidency. Lafitte and his men, who had played a prominent part in the battle, were rewarded by President Madison with full pardons. Lafitte, however, did not choose to remain long in the good graces of the Government: in 1816 he founded yet another pirate colony, Galveztown (Galveston) on the Texas coast, and when this was destroyed in 1821 by an American brig-of-war he fled to Yucatán, where he died in obscurity. Gambi also returned to piracy, and was killed in 1819. Of Lafitte's original lieutenants, only Chinghizola and Dominique You stayed on in New Orleans: the latter died, a much respected citizen, in 1830, and was given a military funeral in St. Louis Cemetery Number One, where his tomb may still be seen.

The losses which the British suffered in the Battle of New Orleans seem even more lamentable when one realizes that the battle was fought just two weeks after the signing of the Treaty of Ghent, which ended hostilities between the two nations: the news had not yet had time to reach these shores by sailing ship, and Pakenham and the soldiers of whom he was so proud (and who comprised an important part of the most powerful and best-trained army on the face of the earth) were thus sacrificed in vain.

[4]

Steamboats had been in occasional use on the Mississippi since 1807, when Robert Fulton designed the *New Orleans,* an ill-fated ship which made only three round trips between Pittsburgh and New Orleans before her boiler exploded—the type of disaster most to be feared with the new kind of vessel. By 1820 there were sixty on the river, and by 1840 there were over four hundred. Steamboat traffic reached its peak in the fifteen years just before the Civil War; after that, the development of railroads caused it to decline.

The earliest vessels had been intended primarily for freight, but as time went on passenger traffic became the more profitable business, and steamboats were built whose chief advantages were comfort, beauty, and, of course, speed. By modern standards they were anything but fast, yet by contrast with sailing ships they must have seemed fleet as the wind. The record for speed on the Mississippi was established by the *Eclipse,* which in 1835 made the trip from New Orleans to Cairo, Illinois, in three days, three hours, and twenty minutes—an average of about fourteen miles per hour. In 1870 the *Robert E. Lee* beat this record by two hours and twenty minutes, yet, as Mark Twain pointed out in *Life on the Mississippi,* the distance between the two cities, owing to the growth of suburbs in the seventeen-year interim, had shrunk to such an extent that the *Eclipse* really made the faster run.

The passenger steamers that were built in the 1830's and 1840's were the last word in elegance. Here at last was a distinctly American achievement, and the builders made the most of it. European palaces were stationary: those of the New World were to float, propelled by the modern miracle of steam. And European visitors were impressed —Thackeray described with enthusiasm a trip he made from New Orleans to Saint Louis in a "huge, tall, white, pasteboard castle of a steamer," and J. C. Flügel, a German visitor, wrote: "The sight of these swimming volcanoes on water is very agreeable. They generally have colors at their poop, and the American eagle and stars give a very handsome effect. A swivel-gun is carried to signalize their arrival and departure." The river steamboat appealed also to the patriotic and aesthetic imagination of American artists and writers, who saw in it a symbol of national greatness and the new age of mechanical progress, as innumerable contemporary canvases (and some of the poems of Walt Whitman) testify. On the Mississippi, the paddle-wheel type popularized by Captain Henry Shreve—after whom Shreveport is named—was the one most commonly seen.

No expense was spared on the furnishings of these ships: they were luxurious beyond anything else known at the time, and the term "steamboat Gothic" has come to mean the ultimate in a particular type of decoration—a type characterized by intricately fretted wood-work on the exterior, and, on the interior, by an abundance of plush and gilt, by chandeliers of glittering bronze and crystal, by deep, soft carpets, and by marble-topped bars of solid mahogany. There was usually a large assortment of vintage wines, the china and silver services were magnificent, and the food was as good as any in America.

Racing and gambling were two traditions early associated with steamboat travel on the Mississippi. There was great rivalry among the various captains where the speed of their ships was concerned, and whenever two steamers of similar type came abreast a race was sure to follow, and crowds often lined the shore to see the result. It was exciting sport but not without its dangerous side, for the boilers were apt to burst when subjected to such unusual strain, and several tragedies had been known to occur in this way: there was the case of the *Washington,* in 1816, with seven fatalities, and, a year later, of the *Constitution,* with twelve. As for gambling, it had existed on the river ever since the days of the flatboat, but it did not achieve the status of an institution until the 1830's. Herbert Asbury has estimated that in the two decades preceding the Civil War there were between six hundred and eight hundred professional gamblers operating on the Mississippi. "Many steamboat captains," he writes, "considered it bad luck to leave a wharf without a gambler on board." Perhaps more often than not, these men were dishonest, but they were among the most colorful types which the period produced—gaudily dressed, with flowered waistcoats and enormous diamond rings. They were not infrequently gifted raconteurs and witty conversationalists, and were sometimes capable of unexpected displays of gallantry and generosity.

The steamboat era, between 1820 and 1850, was the most prosperous in the history of New Orleans. Lloyd's of London prophesied in 1821 that it was destined to become the greatest port in the world, and for a time it looked as if the prophecy was going to be realized. In 1835 her commerce was valued at approximately $54,000,000, while her exports were greater than those of New York; and in 1840 her population was exceeded by only three American cities—New York, Baltimore, and Philadelphia. But New Orleans merchants were not very enterprising; they were content with the *status quo* and with the easy prosperity that resulted from the accident of their location at the gateway of one of the richest agricultural areas in the world. There were almost no warehouses to accommodate the cargoes, which were left outdoors to rot: $100,000 in tobacco was lost in this way in a single season. With the opening of the Erie Canal, in 1825, farmers began shipping their produce east to New York, where it met with a more businesslike reception, and by 1850 New Orleans had lost the lead, even in cotton exports, to the larger city.

Even in her period of greatest affluence, New Orleans was surprisingly backward in many ways—compared, that is, to cities of similar size elsewhere in the nation. Not only were there no covered wharves or warehouses, but there were no central market, no auction rooms, and no exchange until 1833. Only a few streets were paved with cobblestones, and those were mostly uptown, in the American section. There was no municipal lighting system until 1837, and no public sewage disposal until 1892. Sanitary conditions were appalling: John James Audubon, the naturalist, noted in his *Journal* that the French Market was the "dirtiest place in all the cities of the United States."

Educationally, too, New Orleans was slow in developing. The Jeffersonian ideal of free public schools, which after the death of that far-sighted statesman was beginning to prove so influential in other parts of the country, was not shared by many Louisianians. Those who could afford the expense sent their children to private schools, and the wealthier Creoles were in the habit of sending them to France—a tradition that persisted right up to the beginning of the present century. Local opportunities for higher education were particularly limited. The old College of Orleans on Hospital (now Governor Nicholls) Street was founded in 1811 and had a distinguished faculty—it was state-supported and admitted fifty day students and some forty-odd boarders among whom was the historian Charles Gayarré, but it closed its doors in 1826. The first step toward providing adequate public education on all levels was undertaken by the legislature of 1845, which provided for the establishment of free grammar schools throughout the state, as well as for a "University of Louisiana" to be located in New Orleans at the corner of Baronne and Common.

Then as now, New Orleanians seemed more interested in amusements than in civic improvement. Saloons, gambling halls, and bordellos, ranging from elegantly appointed establishments in the French Quarter to the lowest dives in the Girod Street area across Canal Street, did a thriving business. There were several theaters, the oldest being the one on St. Peter Street founded by the Cap Français actors in 1792. Then there was the more impressive St. Philip, which opened in 1808 and which seated seven hundred persons. Uptown, there were the American Theater, opened in 1823 by James Caldwell, and the St. Charles, built in 1835. But the largest of all was the Théâtre d'Orléans, built in 1813 on Orleans Street between Royal and Bourbon; four operas were presented here weekly, and, on the other evenings, vaudeville and musical comedies. Madame Calvé made her American debut here in 1837, and ended by marrying its associate manager, Charles Boudousquié. It was one of the favorite rendezvous of New Orleans society until 1859, when the French Opera House was erected; thereafter the quality of its performances deteriorated, and in 1866 it was destroyed by fire. In the mid-nineteenth century

New Orleans' operatic and theatrical season rivaled that of New York: Jenny Lind, Adelina Patti, and the fabulous Lola Montez were among the many artists who came here for extended engagements.

There were also a number of ballrooms for public dancing. On Condé (now Chartres) Street between St. Ann and Dumaine stood a rather primitive eighteenth century building where, in the early 1800's, the first of the famous quadroon balls took place; later they were held in the St. Philip Theater, and finally, in the 1830's and 1840's, when they enjoyed their greatest popularity, in the magnificent Salle d'Orléans, which adjoined the Théâtre d'Orléans and was said to have the best dance floor in the United States—oak on top of pine.

These quadroon balls were extraordinary affairs. Mulattoes had always had a rather special status in New Orleans society: as the white colonists were responsible for their existence, it was only natural and humane that they should have treated them somewhat differently from full-blooded Negroes. They were referred to as *gens de couleur*, never as *nègres*, and they were seldom slaves; on the contrary, they were frequently slaveowners. (According to Bienville's *Code Noir* they were forbidden to marry either their own slaves or the slaves of whites.) It often happened that when a white man had a child by a Negro slave he would free the mother, and under Louisiana law the child would thus be freed also. A rather rigid hierarchy existed among the *gens de couleur*, based on the amount of white blood in their veins. At the bottom of this hierarchy was the *griffe*, offspring of a Negro and a mulatto, and at the top were the quadroons and octoroons.

The mulatto women were sometimes very beautiful, and it was the ambition of many of them to become the mistresses of well-to-do white men. It is no exaggeration to say that the chief purpose of the quadroon balls, or the *Bals du Cordon Bleu*, as they were properly called, was to provide these girls with an opportunity of meeting men who would become their future lovers. They were not prostitutes, and besides being beautiful were usually well educated and accomplished socially. Harriet Martineau, who visited New Orleans in the 1830's, was very favorably impressed with them. In *Society in America* (1837) she wrote: "The girls are highly educated, externally, and are, probably, as beautiful and accomplished a set of women as can be found. Every young man early selects one, and establishes her in one of those pretty and peculiar houses, whole rows of which may be seen in the Ramparts." The whole thing was elaborately stylized: the gentleman would meet the girl at a ball, declare his affection, and make her an offer. She would refer the matter to her mother, who would inquire into his financial condition ("like a Countess of Kew," wrote Frederick Law Olmsted, another contemporary visitor), and, if satisfied, would require security of him that he would support her daughter adequately and make her a settlement if he should ever leave. Some men continued the relationship even after marriage, having literally two homes.

The quadroon balls, particularly those held in the Salle d'Orléans, were more brilliant than the white balls; the price of admission was twice as high, and attendance was limited to the colored girls, elaborately gowned in the latest fashions and attended invariably by their mothers, and to white gentlemen. They were held twice and sometimes three nights a week, and were reckoned among the sights of the city which no male visitor could afford to miss. There was no rowdiness: the Duke of Saxe-Weimar, who attended some of these functions in the 1830's, observed that they were "much more decent" than the white masquerade balls, and noted that male attendance at the latter suffered sadly when the dates of the two affairs happened to coincide.

But the most permanent and the most popular of the city's many institutions of pleasure was the Mardi Gras, celebrated on the day before Ash Wednesday. This festival, common to Roman Catholic countries in the Mediterranean area, had been brought to Louisiana very early, but it was not until 1838 that the first public parade was organized. Public masking had been banned under the Spanish administration because of the crime with which it had apparently been accompanied, but now it was revived, and the merrymaking was general and unrestrained. Sir Charles Lyell, the geologist, describes as follows a parade which he witnessed in 1846: "There was a great procession parading the streets, almost everyone dressed in the most grotesque attire, troops of them on horseback, some in open carriages, with bands of music, and in a variety of costumes—some as Indians, with feathers in their heads, and one, a jolly, fat man, as Mardi Gras himself. All wore masks, and here and there in the crowd, or stationed in a balcony above, we saw persons armed with bags of flour, which they showered down copiously on any one who seemed particularly fond of his attire."

The old rivalry between Creoles and Americans, though diminished by the Battle of New Orleans, did not die out altogether, and was responsible for slowing down municipal progress—one reason why New Orleans did not keep pace with other cities. There was constant friction between the two elements, and in 1836 the state legislature attempted an experiment which was unique in American city government: it issued a charter dividing New Orleans into three independent municipalities, each presided over by a recorder and a council. The charter also provided for a mayor and a general council who was to exercise certain general supervisory powers, but these powers were largely nominal; in effect, New Orleans was now three cities with separate corporate rights and (oddest of all) with separate currencies. The First Municipality, which was also the seat of the mayor and general council, was the Vieux Carré; the Second Municipality was the new uptown section across Canal Street; and the Third was the area below Esplanade Avenue, the old Faubourg Marigny, which had been part of Bernard de Marigny's plantation. According to this scheme, which proved extremely cumbersome, the Creoles outnumbered the Americans two to one in matters of civic administration, but the Second Municipality was constantly growing in size, wealth, and prestige. When, in 1852, the three-city form of government was abandoned, and the mayor and his council moved from the Cabildo to the new City Hall on Lafayette Square, the ascendancy of the Americans was at last established.

Unfortunately, the new order was characterized by corruption from the very beginning: machines dominated the city's politics, and graft, nepotism, and demagoguery came to be the order of the day. The period just before the Civil War was, politically, one of the worst in the city's history. In 1856 the Native American or Know-Nothing party, a national organization whose program in New Orleans called for the destruction of Creole and foreign influence in the city, elected Charles M. Waterman mayor by seizing the polling places and intimidating voters. On June 1, 1858, the Know-Nothings stole the registration lists and struck off the names of non-party members, an outrage which resulted in the formation of a Vigilance Committee, a group of nearly a thousand conscientious citizens who proceeded to take matters into their own hands. Headed by Captain Johnson Duncan, they seized the Cabildo and the State Arsenal, and barricaded themselves in the French Quarter. Mayor Waterman ordered them to disband, but Duncan replied that they would do so only on condition that the mayor authorize them to act as special policemen at the forthcoming election. This Waterman at first refused to do; in order to avert bloodshed, however, he was at last obliged to accept Duncan's terms, though doing so caused him to lose face with his own party to such an extent that he later resigned. The elections were held in an orderly manner, but the Know-Nothings were victorious and remained in office until the Civil War. During this period the prestige of the Creoles in New Orleans was naturally at its very lowest ebb.

Canal Street was the boundary between two worlds. Alexander Mackay wrote in 1847: "You not only, in crossing Canal Street, seem to bound from one century to another, but you might also fancy that you had crossed the boundary line between two coterminous nations." The rallying point of the Americans was the St. Charles Hotel, which, when it was opened in 1837, was hyperbolically considered one of the architectural wonders of the century, standing in the same relation to New Orleans (as a contemporary journalist observed) as the Parthenon to Athens, Notre Dame to Paris, and St. Mark's to Venice. It was twice destroyed by fire, in 1851 and 1894, and rebuilt; the present hotel is the third to occupy the site. The Creoles were not long in retaliating with the St. Louis Hotel, an even more impressive building constructed on the corner of Royal and St. Louis which immediately became the center of social life in the Vieux Carré: subscription balls of great magnificence were held here, and, later, many of the Mardi Gras balls. In 1874 the building was sold to the state and served as the Capitol of Louisiana; it was demolished in 1914. Where hotels were concerned, at any rate, New Orleans was not backward: the St. Charles and the St. Louis were the best in America, and had no real rivals until the Astor House was built in New York several years later.

New Orleans' greatest nemesis in the nineteenth century was yellow fever. It had occurred in waves almost from the founding of the city, and there were two things about it which puzzled the medical authorities: it would usually strike in summer, and the natives were less likely to be attacked than newcomers, the greatest mortality rate occurring among sailors and immigrants—as high as fifty per cent in some years. It was supposed therefore that the heat had something to do with it, and that the natives had built up a kind of immunity: both assumptions were correct, but seemed to lead nowhere. It was also believed to be contagious—which it is not—and all sorts of fantastic measures (such as the burning of chemicals and barrels of tar, and the firing of cannon loaded with gunpowder) were adopted in vain. Not until the early 1900's was it known that the carrier was the female mosquito of the Stegomyia species. Asiatic cholera was another menace, and the two diseases raged simultaneously in the terrible epidemics of 1832–1833 and 1853, killing both visitors and natives at an alarming rate: in the former year, 10,000 deaths were reported; in the latter, 40,000. These figures are the more appalling when one realizes that during the summer months many thousands of inhabitants were in the custom of leaving the city for the northern shore of Lake Pontchartrain and elsewhere at the first sign of an epidemic (thus, in 1832, out of a permanent population of 80,000 only 25,000 remained in the city) and that nearly a third of the total population succumbed.

New Orleans presented a fearful sight during these two epidemics. Wagons were driven through the streets to collect the corpses, which were so numerous that, since it was necessary to bury them above ground in vaults, it was impossible to dispose of them immediately. In the cemeteries, coffins were heaped high in rows, awaiting burial; some of them were of the most primitive construction, and, thus exposed to the elements, quickly decayed: the stench, according to contemporary accounts, was almost unbearable. The inhabitants of whole sections of the city were wiped out. The Reverend Theodore Clapp, who left an eyewitness report of the 1853 epidemic, wrote: "In some cases all the clerks and agents belonging to mercantile establishments were swept away and the stores closed by the civil authorities. Several entire families were carried off—parents, children, servants, all. Others lost a quarter, or a third, or three-fourths of their members, and their business, hopes and happiness were blasted for life."

Another mid-century disaster in the New Orleans vicinity, though on a smaller scale, was the destruction of Last Island by a hurricane on August 10, 1856. This island, which lies off the Louisiana coast, had become a fashionable pleasure resort not only with New Orleanians but with visitors from all over the state and even outside it; it was beginning to be known as the Newport of the South, and contained several hotels, the largest of which was the Trade Wind, a huge building fronting 1,250 feet on the beach. The hurricane struck at the height of the tourist season, destroying all the buildings on the island and later submerging them with a gigantic tidal wave. During the storm a ball was in progress at the Trade Wind, but the gaiety of the dancers changed to panic as they saw water seeping up through the ballroom floor: soon the entire building was inundated and swept away. Approximately three hundred persons lost their lives in this hurricane. When the waves at last receded, looters came in droves, but there was very little left of value on Last Island. Bodies continued to be washed ashore for days, some of them grotesquely attired in ballroom finery. The incident provided Lafcadio Hearn with the inspiration for *Chita*, which is probably the best nineteenth century novel dealing with Louisiana. Last Island was never rebuilt. There is absolutely nothing on it today, and so strong was the memory of this catastrophe that only in recent years have attempts been made to establish resorts on neighboring islands.

New Orleans was much excited by a number of filibustering expeditions against Cuba and Central America, for which it was the logical port of embarkation. The leaders of these campaigns were usually professional adventurers and demagogues, motivated not so much by patriotic sentiment as by a craving for fame and easy fortune. Strictly speaking, any filibustering activity was in direct violation of the neutrality laws of 1818, yet so shrewdly did these men plan their operations that the popular press was often on their side, and there was never any lack of volunteers. To a modern reader it seems strange that they were seldom brought to official justice, and that when they were they were usually acquitted; but it was an era of individual enterprise, and the government for the most part was indulgent. One of the most popular filibusters was Narciso López, a Venezuelan who had so distinguished himself in Spain that in 1839 he received a major general's commission and was appointed Governor of Valencia. In 1841 he left Spain for Cuba, where he became involved with a revolutionary party working for the annexation of that island to the United States. When his disloyalty was discovered he escaped to this country, where he was encouraged by Governor Quitman and Senator Henderson, of Mississippi, to raise an expedition to liberate Cuba. In New Orleans he raised an army of about six hundred men, many of them veterans of the Mexican War, and took them to Yucatán for a brief training period. On May 19, 1850, he landed his men at the Cuban port of Cárdenas, where he expected to meet the Cuban underground, but somehow the plan miscarried and after suffering heavy losses he was obliged to flee to Key West. No sooner was he back in the United States than he began raising funds for another, more carefully organized invasion. He issued bonds (many of which were sold in New Orleans) to be redeemed at a six per cent rate after the Spanish were expelled from the island, and in order to attract volunteers promised to pay five thousand dollars to every soldier as soon as the invasion had been successfully concluded. This time there were to be three armies instead of one: the other two were to be headed by General Ambrosio Gonzáles, a Washington lawyer sympathetic to the cause of the insurgents, and the other by Governor Quitman. López was to be in charge of the entire expedition, and he offered the command of his own troops first to Jefferson Davis (then a United States senator) and then to Major Robert E. Lee, but neither was interested.

López' army of about four hundred and fifty men was ready by July 1, 1851, but Gonzáles' and Quitman's troops were not yet fully recruited or prepared. Meanwhile the wily governor of Cuba, Don José Gutierrez de la Concha, aware of López' impatience and hoping to lure him to the island before he could be joined by the other expeditions, caused reports to be circulated in New Orleans that the insurgents had rebelled in various cities and had driven out the Spanish. There was great excitement in the city at this news: mass meetings were held in Lafayette Square and at Banks' Arcade (a favorite rendezvous with filibusters) at which various popular speakers declared that this was the moment to strike, and the newspapers echoed this opinion. López fell for the trap; he and his men sailed from New Orleans on August 3rd on board the *Pampero*. Landing at Bahía Honda, they were attacked by a large Spanish force and annihilated: López himself was captured and executed in Havana on September 1st. The popularity in New Orleans of this extraordinary man was such that at the news of his death a mob gathered and wrecked the office of *La Unión*, the city's Spanish newspaper, as well as the Spanish consulate and a number of Spanish-owned coffeehouses and tobacco stores.

The career of William Walker is even more remarkable. A Tennesseean educated at Heidelberg, he had already conducted two filibustering expeditions in northern Mexico when some American businessmen interested him in Nicaragua, where there was actually some revolutionary activity in progress. In May, 1855, he sailed with only fifty-eight men for Rialejo, on the northern coast, where he was joined by 170 insurgents. Walker was luckier than López—for a time. He captured the city of Granada, and when this information reached the United States his agents made the most of it: advertisements appeared in the newspapers calling for volunteers, and approximately 1,500 men responded. Soon Walker was in control of the country, and the government which he established there, with himself as President, was recognized officially by President Franklin Pierce. His administration, however, proved so unpopular that in May, 1857, only two years after he had effected his coup, he was forced to return to the United States. He set up residence on Customhouse (now Iberville) Street and was arrested there, somewhat tardily, for violating the neutrality laws. Having been released on bail, he sailed again for Nicaragua in November, 1857, with 132 men but was soon apprehended by Commodore Hiram Paulding and returned to New York for trial. President James Buchanan, however, declaring that his arrest on foreign soil was illegal, refused to prosecute. In June, 1860, he led yet a third filibustering expedition, this time to Honduras. It was his last: on September 12th he met his death at the hands of a firing squad in Trujillo.

Though men like López and Walker were certainly not motivated by lofty ideals, they were natural leaders of men, able and ambitious —individuals who, in different circumstances and with more effective backing, might easily have left permanent marks on the history of the New World. Not so with the men whom they attracted: these were composed for the most part of riffraff, vagrants, and ne'er-do-wells— but not entirely. There is in every society a class of men, usually young men, for whom the legitimate excitements of civilized life are insufficient. Wars on a national scale provide such men as these with an outlet for their passions, besides giving them the stamp of social approval, but in times of peace they must take their excitement where they can find it, and even manufacture it upon occasion. Filibustering appealed strongly to men of this temperament.

Another outlet for high-spirited young men was dueling, which was more widely practiced in New Orleans during the first half of the nineteenth century than in any other city in North America. The custom originated in the previous century among the Creoles, who brought it with them from Europe, and reached its maximum popularity between 1830 and 1840; it died out, like so many other customs in the South, with the Civil War. The rivalry between Creoles and Americans after the Louisiana Purchase was productive of many duels, as were also the quadroon balls: Herbert Asbury writes that "the Creole was even quicker to resent a fancied slight or insult to his colored mistress than to his white wife or fiancée." The Creoles preferred swords and pistols, but the Americans sometimes dueled with rifles and shotguns. Rapiers were probably the most popular weapon, and in 1840 there were more than fifty fencing academies in the city, centered mostly in and about Exchange Alley, which runs from Canal to Conti between Royal and Chartres streets. Some of the more renowned teachers, like Pepe Lulla, a Catalan; Gilbert Rosière, a Frenchman; and Bastile Cròquière, a mulatto, enjoyed enormous local prestige, and, rather like the juke-box idols of today, had enormous followings of fans.

The authorities tried to suppress dueling, even introducing a clause into the state constitution in 1848 which disfranchised the participants, but public reaction to this law was so unfavorable that four years later it was repealed. The custom naturally came in for a good bit of satire (Walt Whitman ridiculed it in a sketch, "Daggerdraw Bowieknife, Esq.," which he published in 1848 in the New Orleans *Daily Crescent*), but it was so thoroughly established in the city that nothing could discourage it: in 1837 ten duels were fought on a single Sunday under the oak trees at Louis Allard's plantation, now City Park; this and St. Anthony's Square, behind the cathedral, were the favorite places. It was not easy for a gentleman in public life to avoid dueling at least once in his career: Governor Claiborne himself was no exception— in 1806 he quarreled with the territorial delegate to Washington, Daniel Clark, who shot him through the right thigh in a secret meeting.

[5]

The Civil War period is not a very momentous one in the history of New Orleans. No important battles were fought in or around it, and in this respect it differs from other large Southern cities like Atlanta or Richmond. The reason, of course, is that it was occupied by Federal troops early in the war and remained so occupied until hostilities ended. And yet, because of its size and importance, New Orleans stood to lose more from a Southern defeat than most cities: when Louisiana seceded from the Union on January 26, 1861, New Orleans was the fourth largest city in the nation, and her total commerce (forty-five per cent of which was in cotton) stood at $324,-000,000. She was never to recover this prestige.

Secession had the effect of uniting the Creoles and the Americans just as in the War of 1812, only now the union was more complete and more permanent. Both elements responded eagerly to the call for volunteers, and the New Orleans contingent, which included several Zouave companies wearing scarlet fezzes and baggy Moroccan trousers, was the most colorful in the Confederacy. One of the most brilliant Southern generals, Pierre Gustave Toutant Beauregard, was a Creole from St. Bernard Parish, just outside the city: when Louisiana seceded he was serving as superintendent of West Point, a post he immediately resigned in order to serve the Confederacy.

Early in the war the Federal Government decided to blockade the Gulf ports, and stationed cruisers at the mouth of the Mississippi, thus shutting off the ocean trade upon which the prosperity of the city so largely depended. In March, 1862, the North began its preparations for seizing New Orleans by sending a fleet of forty-three ships commanded by Admiral David Glasgow Farragut to Ship Island, in the Mississippi Sound, where the soldiers whom it transported (twenty thousand strong) underwent a five-week period under General Benjamin F. Butler, who was to assume authority over the captured city. New Orleans was guarded rather inadequately by two forts, Fort Jackson and Fort St. Philip, located on opposite sides of the river about seventy miles south of the city, and below these by a large chain stretched across the river and buoyed by the hulks of eleven schooners. Within the city there were only three thousand regular soldiers and a few battalions of militia; most of the troops raised in New Orleans had been sent to fight elsewhere.

On April 18th Farragut's fleet began bombarding the forts, and two days later he succeeded in snapping the chain. On the night of April 24th he slipped past the forts, and steamed up to New Orleans. General Lovell, who commanded the troops in the city, had wisely evacuated them, and had ordered all the cotton and tobacco burned: when the Federals landed, the sky above the city was black with smoke, and it is estimated that over $1,000,000 of cotton was thus destroyed on wharves and in warehouses. There was no organized resistance, but when the Union flag was hoisted (a bit prematurely, as the city had not yet formally surrendered), a group of young men tore it down; one of them, William Mumford, was later hanged by Butler for his participation in this incident. The execution nearly caused a riot in the city, and enraged Jefferson Davis, who issued a proclamation declaring that Butler was not merely an enemy of the Confederacy but "an outlaw and common enemy of mankind," and ordering his immediate execution by hanging in the event of capture.

Butler made himself disliked in many ways. In August, 1862, he disarmed all the citizens, and in September of the same year he ordered all New Orleanians over eighteen either to take the oath of allegiance to the Federal Government under penalty of fine or imprisonment at hard labor or to register as enemies of the Union and go to live within the Confederate lines. Butler's biggest problem, however, was with the women of New Orleans, who were more flagrant than the males in showing their hatred of the occupation. Butler himself describes an incident which occurred as he and some other officers were riding past a balcony: "Just as we were passing the balcony, with something like a shriek and a sneer, the women all whirled around with a flirt which threw out their skirts in a regular circle like the pirouette of a dancer. I turned to my aide, saying in a full voice: 'Those women evidently know which end of them looks best.'"

Some women had even gone so far as to spit on the Union soldiers, and Butler was at his wits' end to find a remedy for the situation. At last he drafted his so-called Woman's Order, which read: "As the officers and soldiers of the United States have been subjected to repeated insults from the women (calling themselves ladies) of New Orleans, in return for the most scrupulous non-interference and courtesy on our part, it is ordered that hereafter when any female shall, by word, gesture, or movement, insult or show contempt for any officer or soldier of the United States, she shall be regarded and held liable to be treated as a woman of the town plying her profession." Of all Butler's moves, this one proved the most unwise. Southern chivalry was outraged, and he was also criticized in the North: even the London press was indignant. But Butler remained firm: when Mayor John T. Monroe protested, he had him arrested and installed General George Shepley of Maine in his place; henceforth the city was under martial law. In December, 1862, Butler was relieved of his command, partly because of pressure from foreign consuls in New Orleans whom he had antagonized; and Nathaniel Banks, former governor of Massachusetts, assumed control of the city.

Butler's character has been the subject of much controversy. He has been maligned by Southern historians, looting and profiteering being the principal charges (he is said to have been particularly fond of silver, and the sobriquet "Silver Spoon Butler," as well as the less flattering "Beast Butler," still persists in the local references), but it must be remembered that during the Civil War profiteering was common on both sides, and that Butler's position as officer in charge of a conquered city was not an enviable one. He apparently lacked the necessary tact and judgment for such a post, but he was not lacking in efficiency: the manner in which he attended to the feeding of the population, which when he assumed command of the city had been reduced by the blockade almost to the point of starvation, was thoroughly businesslike, as was also the manner in which he flushed and drained the city streets. Probably Butler's greatest fault was a certain obstinacy: having made up his mind on a particular course, he was determined not to deviate from it, even when to do so would have been the better part of discretion. (One senses this in his account of Mumford's execution, where it is apparent that he persisted in his intention mainly because of his determination to prove that he was not, as was popularly supposed, merely bluffing.)

When the Civil War ended, most New Orleanians felt a sense of relief; under military government the city had suffered morally, if not physically, and though the loss of their slaves was a severe economic blow the prospect of once more being their own masters was a welcome one. Lincoln had drafted a lenient postwar policy according to which the Southern states were to be readmitted as soon as ten per cent of the voting population of 1860 would pledge loyalty to the Union, and he proposed to pardon all Southerners who did this with the exception of certain Confederate leaders. He did not plan to extend franchise to the liberated Negroes immediately and indiscriminately, and in this position he was supported by most Northern intellectuals: Louis Agassiz of Harvard had written in 1863, while the war was still in progress: "I cannot, therefore, think it just or safe to grant at once to the Negro all the privileges which we ourselves have acquired by long struggles." He added prophetically: "History teaches us what terrible reactions have followed too extensive and too rapid changes." Lincoln was in favor of deporting the freedmen, and the nearest he ever came to proposing Negro franchise was in a letter to Michael Hahn, governor of Louisiana during Federal occupation: "I barely suggest, for your private consideration, whether some of the colored people may not be let in, as for instance, the very intelligent, and especially those who have fought gallantly in our ranks. They would probably help, in some trying time to come, to keep the jewel of liberty within the family of freedom. But this is only a suggestion, not to the public, but to you alone." In his last public speech, the President pleaded for a liberal reconstruction, and on the day before his death, April 14th, he held a cabinet meeting at which he did likewise.

Lincoln's conservatism, however, was not shared by all of Congress, and after his assassination his policy was attacked with fresh vigor by the Radical Republicans, who had consistently opposed him. These, led by Thaddeus Stevens, demanded that the South should be treated as a conquered foreign province. "Settle the Southern states with new men," he declared, "and exterminate or drive out the present rebels as exiles." The policy of Andrew Johnson, who succeeded Lincoln, was essentially like that of his predecessor, except that he advocated the confiscation of Southern estates as the most effective means of destroying the old "slaveocracy," and he defended this policy unsuccessfully against the Radicals, who managed to contrive his impeachment: he escaped conviction by a single vote. These men, who foresaw an end to the Republican party if Southern state governments were restored with representation in Washington, refused to recognize these representatives when, the Southern states having duly "reconstructed" themselves along the liberal lines laid out by Washington and Johnson, they were at last elected. Johnson fought the Radicals for a year, but in the end they had their way: the new civil governments in the Southern states were declared unconstitutional, and by the harsh Reconstruction Act of 1867 the whole South was divided into five military districts supervised by major-generals. Ratification of the Fourteenth Amendment, which gave franchise to the Negro at the same time that it removed it from the white leaders who had participated in the rebellion, was made a condition of readmission to the Union: this proved a shrewd move on the part of the Radicals, for in 1868, when their candidate, Ulysses S. Grant, ran for President he was elected by a Negro majority of 700,000 over Horatio Seymour, the Democratic candidate.

In New Orleans, the feeling of relief attendant upon the cessation of hostilities and the prospect of self-government changed to one of dismay, which increased when the city began to fill up with Northern adventurers whom the Radicals had encouraged to go South, where they were immediately enfranchised with the understanding that they would support the Republican party; these men, known as Carpet-baggers, soon gained control of the state government, together with the newly enfranchised Negroes and a scattering of Scalawags, which was a term applied to the few Southerners who threw in their lot with the Radicals. The Carpetbag politicians, who had no property in the state (or anywhere else, for that matter—the name was applied to them because it was said they carried all their possessions in their carpetbags, a type of suitcase popular in the middle of the century), had only one interest, and that was to get rich as quickly as possible: they levied exorbitant property taxes, from which they themselves did not stand to suffer, and through their extravagance increased the public debt of Louisiana by forty million dollars. During the period when the state legislature was controlled by Carpetbaggers, Negroes, and Scalawags, political corruption in the state reached a new peak. The situation in Louisiana was particularly serious, owing to the size of the Negro population, and ex-slaves, many of them illiterates who only a few years previously had toiled in the fields, now held high offices and actually outnumbered the whites in the legislature. The second highest office in the state, that of lieutenant-governor, was held by a Negro, Oscar J. Dunn, and the governor was Henry Clay Warmoth, who declared quite openly: "I do not pretend to be honest, only as honest as anybody in politics."

Presently the Republicans began to quarrel among themselves. Warmoth was impeached; when he retired (with a large fortune), he was succeeded by a Negro governor, P. B. S. Pinchback, and finally by a Carpetbagger, William P. Kellogg. Some of the more intelligent Negroes, realizing that the Carpetbaggers were interested in enriching themselves rather than in improving the lot of the colored race (bands of emancipated Negroes roamed the state looking in vain for the "mule and forty acres" which the Republicans had promised them), switched to the Democratic party, and in the election of 1874 the Democrats actually won the vote, but a returning board composed of Carpetbaggers declared a Republican victory.

Resistance to Carpetbaggery in New Orleans was organized in the form of a "White League," and on September 14, 1874, a battle took place in the streets between members of this group and Kellogg's metropolitan police force. Forty men were killed and a hundred wounded in this skirmish, which resulted in a temporary victory for the League; President Grant was obliged to dispatch General Philip H. Sheridan to subdue the citizens and restore Kellogg to office. The Carpetbag régime in the South had for some time been under attack from Northern intellectuals and from the press, and they now redoubled their efforts. Wrote the Chicago *Times:* "The rebellion in the city of New Orleans is one of the full-grown fruits of that most unwise and short-sighted statesmanship which, refusing to deal with human nature as it is, proceeded upon the assumption that it is possible to reconstruct human nature by force of Congressional enactments. Not the cool judgment of wise heads, but the hot passions of hate and revenge inspired the Reconstruction policy of the Washington Congress, whose fruits of violence, butchery, and revolutionary outbreaks the Southern half of the republic has ever since been harvesting."

As early as 1872 it was apparent to Congress that radical reconstruction was a failure, and in that year the Radicals granted amnesty to all ex-Confederates. But it was too late—the Republican party had doomed itself in the South. Gradually the states won back self-government, forming the Democratic alliance known as the Solid South. Louisiana, however, was one of the last to do so: if New Orleans had been spared the horrors of the actual war, she experienced to the fullest the horrors that followed it. It was not until 1876 that the Democrats succeeded in electing their gubernatorial candidate, Francis T. Nicholls. The following year President Rutherford B. Hayes withdrew Federal troops from the city, and the long decade of interference and misrule came to an end. In 1879 a new state constitution was drawn up which restricted Negro votes by increasing the appointive power of the governor and the qualifications for admission to the legislature, and in 1898 a convention was called which imposed educational and property qualifications for voters; as a result, many Negroes were disfranchised.

[6]

New Orleans revived slowly from the effects of Reconstruction. The biggest single step toward economic recovery was the construction in 1879 of a system of jetties by Captain James B. Eads which permanently deepened the mouth of the Mississippi, making it possible for large ocean-going vessels to pass freely. This necessitated an increase of port facilities, which in its turn was followed by railroad expansion. In 1873 the Illinois Central Railroad established through service to Chicago, and by 1880 the city was served by no fewer than five trunk lines; in 1883, when it was joined to the West Coast by the Southern Pacific Railroad, rail service was established to all parts of the country. As the port expanded, the city extended her boundaries to include Algiers and Jefferson City, which in 1870 became the fifth and sixth districts respectively, and Carrollton, which became the seventh.

The cotton trade revived, and in 1884 and 1885 the World's Industrial and Cotton Centennial Exposition was held in New Orleans; its purpose was partly to stimulate Southern industry in general, partly to advertise the newly expanded port, and partly to celebrate a century of growth in international cotton trade, which had increased from the single bale exported to England in 1784 to a total of four million bales for foreign consumption. It was held on the present site of Audubon Park, and its main building, which covered thirty-three acres, was the largest of its kind ever built—bigger by 250,000 square feet than London's Crystal Palace. The fair grounds were lighted by electricity, and this was the first large-scale public display of it in New Orleans: electric lights had been installed on Canal Street in 1882 and on Royal Street two years later, but this was a feeble spectacle compared to the four thousand incandescent and 1,100 standard arc lamps which lighted up the Exposition area. Visitors from all over the United States and from many foreign countries came to marvel at this and other wonders of the machine age.

Journalism became accelerated. The afternoon *Daily Item* (which as the *New Orleans Item* continued publication as late as 1958) was founded in 1877: Lafcadio Hearn joined its staff the following year and served for a time as chief editorial writer. The *Daily States* began in 1880, and in 1881 the *Daily Democrat* and the older *Daily Times* merged into the *Times-Democrat*, which in 1914 combined with the oldest of them all, the *New Orleans Picayune*, to form the present *Times-Picayune*.

There was also a revival of education. Negroes had been admitted to the public schools during Reconstruction, with the result that white parents withdrew their children; some of them entered private academies, but the majority received no instruction whatever. In the late 1870's, the New Orleans public school system was restored, and in 1884 a free night school was opened by the same Sophie B. Wright who, five years later, founded the Home Institute on Camp Street, a private school for girls. Also in 1884 the old Louisiana University was expanded into Tulane University by means of a donation of more than a million dollars from Paul Tulane, and in 1886 the Sophie New-comb College for girls, which later became a part of Tulane, was founded by Mrs. Josephine Newcomb.

There was much controversy in New Orleans in the late 1880's concerning the Louisiana Lottery, a state-authorized institution whose charter had been obtained from the corrupt Carpetbag legislature (for a price) in 1886; according to its terms the company which controlled the lottery was exempted from taxation provided it con-tributed $40,000 annually to the support of Charity Hospital. The lottery had always been opposed by churchmen and reformers, who referred to it as the "Golden Octopus," and in 1879 the legislature, which no longer considered itself bound by the Carpetbag constitu-tion, repealed the charter, whereupon Charles T. Howard and John Morris, the partners who controlled the lottery, offered to pay the state an annual sum of $1,250,000 if it would reverse its decision. The legislature reconsidered and finally granted the company a fifteen-year extension. During this period, from 1879 to 1895, the Louisiana Lottery enjoyed its greatest prosperity: it grossed thirty million dollars a year, and some of its profits went into such civic works as the repairing of levees, maintenance of the French Opera House, and the support of Carnival. Nevertheless, opposition con-tinued to mount; there was national as well as local criticism, and a Federal law was passed which forbade lotteries from advertising and from sending tickets through the mails. When Francis T. Nicholls campaigned for a second term as governor he denounced the institu-tion, and when, at the expiration of its charter, the legislature voted for its renewal, Nicholls vetoed their action; a referendum was then taken to the people, who voted it out of existence.

In the 1880's large numbers of Sicilian immigrants began arriving in the city; the majority of these were law-abiding individuals to whom the biggest objection was that, since they were willing to work for very low wages, they increased economic competition, and there was some resentment in New Orleans against them on this score. Among them, however, were several refugees from justice—members of the Mafia, a secret organization, originally political, which had been outlawed in Italy, and their arrival in America inaugurated a tradition of gang-style violence and terrorism which still persists in cities of this country where the Sicilian element is largest. A young New Orleans policeman, David Hennessy, had attracted some atten-tion by capturing one of the Mafia leaders, a man named Esposito, who was wanted for murder in Italy. Esposito was deported and executed, and Hennessy, who had refused bribes amounting to fifty thousand dollars for his release, henceforth became a marked man. For this and other achievements he was promoted in the force, finally becoming Chief of Police.

In 1891 a feud existed between two Sicilian families, the Provenzanos and the Matrangas, for control of waterfront labor: there had been several shootings, and Hennessy was determined to bring the lawbreakers to justice. He had secured evidence that the leaders of the Matranga faction were members of the Mafia, and was on the verge of disclosing this evidence when he was shot on his doorstep by a group of assassins who pumped six bullets into his body from a sawed-off shotgun. The city was outraged, and no effort was spared to locate the criminals. As it happened, there were several clues, and so skillfully did the police follow them up that within four days six suspects had been arrested. Altogether, eighteen men were involved in the crime, and the state, assisted by the famous detective James B. Pinkerton, who came to the city for the purpose, built up an elaborate case against nine of them. The Italians, however, some of whom were wealthy men, had hired influential attorneys, and it was obvious, when the jury acquitted six of the defendants and declared a mistrial in the case of the others, that its members had been "fixed." Popular resentment against the Italians and the jury which had acquitted them now mounted to fever pitch; no one talked of anything else. The following day, a notice appeared in the morning papers summoning "all good citizens" to attend a mass meeting that evening "to remedy the failure of justice in the Hennessy case." A mob gathered, marched to the parish prison in Congo Square where the prisoners were awaiting release, broke down the door, shot nine of them, and hanged two others. The lynching attracted international attention: Italy lodged an official protest, and even withdrew her minister from Washington, obliging President Benjamin Harrison, who deplored the killings as an "offense against law and humanity," to reassure that country that the incident did not reflect the feeling of Americans toward the Italian people as a whole. An indemnity of $25,000 was eventually paid to Italy by the United States Government.

Louisiana was one of the first states in the Union to legalize prize fighting; it did so in 1890, and for the next twenty years New Orleans was the national center for this sport. In 1892 three world championship fights were held in three successive evenings at the Olympic

Club, and in one of them, James J. Corbett took the heavyweight title away from John L. Sullivan by a knockout in the twenty-first round. The longest fight in the history of boxing (seven hours and fourteen minutes) took place here on April 6, 1893, between Andy Bowen and Jack Burke, as did also the first glove-fought contest, between Louis Nuckols and Charles Carroll. The New Orleans area has produced three world champions: Pete Herman, who now runs a night club on Bourbon Street; Tony Canzoneri; and Joe Brown, the present lightweight titleholder.

In the 1880's and 1890's prostitution was more active in New Orleans than in any other American city. Brothels were springing up all over town, even in the politer neighborhoods, and the more respectable citizens protested vigorously. In 1897 an alderman, Sidney Story, proposed a plan for setting up a red-light district covering thirty-eight squares and limiting prostitution in New Orleans to this area; his plan was adopted, and, when brothel-keepers in other neighborhoods challenged it, was upheld by the Louisiana Supreme Court. Basin Street was the principal thoroughfare of this district, which (to the embarrassment of its planner) came to be known thereafter as Storyville, and on it were erected the biggest and the most elaborate of the new bordellos. Some of them, like Josie Arlington's place ("Château Lobrano d'Arlington") and the establishments run by Lulu White and "Countess" Willie Piazza, both octoroons, were very elegantly appointed and numbered among their clientele some of the richest and most influential men in New Orleans. There were statues, paintings, Oriental carpets, antique furniture, and, of course, mirrors in the bedroom ceilings: the Countess Piazza even had a music box installed in her mattress.

Storyville quickly became one of the sights of the city. It has been estimated that as many as two thousand women operated within its limits, and the numerous bars, restaurants, and dance halls also did a rushing business: profits were enormous. Of course the police took their share, for though prostitution was legal in the district a house could be raided for disturbance, and this was easy to arrange. The acknowledged boss of Storyville was a man named Tom Anderson, whose mistress was Josie Arlington: he owned three big saloons of which the most pretentious, known as Arlington Annex, served as semiofficial headquarters of the district. Anderson was, in effect, the mayor of Storyville, and was recognized as such by City Hall, which passed on to him matters concerning the peace of the neighborhood.

With the blessing of the city authorities, he did a thing which is unique in the history of American cities, and that is to publish an annual *Blue Book* of the red-light district, which was a Who's Who of the various houses, listing their addresses, their telephone numbers, the names of the madams and the more popular prostitutes. There were comments on the specialties of each establishment, many pages of advertisements, and an abundance of photographs. Copies of this extraordinary directory are still to be seen occasionally in the local bookshops; they have become collectors' items.

Storyville has a certain cultural importance in the history of New Orleans and of the nation, for it was on the pianos of the brothels and honky-tonks of this neighborhood that early jazz techniques were being explored by such artists as "Jelly Roll" Morton, who played the big white piano in Mahogany Hall, Lulu White's house. The very earliest jazz was played on wind instruments by pioneers like Buddy Bolden and Bunk Johnson, whose styles on the cornet had matured as early as 1895 and who played in the numerous street parades of the Negro organizations to which they belonged: after the creation of Storyville, however, whose many establishments afforded unprecedented opportunity for Negro musicians (and especially for pianists, as the madams preferred music which was relatively quiet), the piano began to monopolize the medium, and it is a fact that most jazz forms have been developed on that instrument. There was not a single brothel or bar of any importance in Storyville that did not have its "professor" at the piano.

[7]

In 1800 the population of New Orleans was less than ten thousand; in 1900 it was 287,104. The new century was to witness further growth, though not at so sensational a rate. The twentieth century in New Orleans has mainly been a period of industrial and commercial expansion, and of much-needed civic improvement. Nor did the city escape the clashes between labor and capital which were the reaction to an era of unprecedented and often unbridled enterprise: streetcar employees struck unsuccessfully for shorter hours and higher wages in 1902, and five years later eight thousand dockworkers gained certain concessions by means of a general walkout.

In 1904 a highly efficient water purification system replaced the old family cistern, and it was not long before open sewers were abandoned for modern underground mains; there were also improvements in the drainage system. The last yellow-fever epidemic occurred in 1905—since then the disease has been under control and is now relatively rare. There was progress in education, too: Loyola University was built in 1911, and in the same year two large girls' high schools, Sophie B. Wright and John McDonogh, were erected; Warren Easton, the boys' high school on Canal Street, was constructed in 1913. (These high schools have since become coeducational.) In politics, the city aldermen were replaced by the commission form of government in 1912.

During World War I a number of military camps were established in New Orleans, and as a result of pressure from military and naval authorities Storyville was closed down: there had been several violent incidents involving servicemen and a number of them had contracted venereal disease there. There was much criticism of this action, however, and Mayor Martin Behrman even made a hurried trip to Washington for the purpose of restraining it. The war had a decidedly sobering effect upon the city: even the Carnival was suspended in 1918 and 1919.

From the very date of its founding, New Orleans had been threatened by floods from the Mississippi, and in the terrible flood year of 1927 (when property damage in the Delta amounted to $236,000,000), only a few inches separated the water level from the top of the levees which protected the city. There was much excitement, and at last it was decided to dynamite the levee several miles below the city, flooding an area whose value was relatively insignificant: this was done, the water level sank at the city proper, and New Orleans was saved from destruction.

Politics in Louisiana in the late twenties and early thirties were dominated by Huey P. Long, who was governor from 1928 to 1932 and United States senator from 1932 to 1935. Long was a controversial figure in his lifetime, and the controversy did not end with his death: opinion in the state is still sharply divided on the subject of his administration, which was productive of benefits and evils in almost equal proportion. The man who was to become the undisputed dictator of Louisiana was born in Winn Parish, in the northwestern part of the state, the eighth of nine children. The family was a poor one: Huey had to borrow money to go to Tulane, where he completed the three-year law course in eight months and was permitted to take the bar examination, which he passed brilliantly (his memory was phenomenal) only after he had secured a special permit from the Chief Justice of the Louisiana Supreme Court—the persuasiveness of his personality had already begun to prevail over obstacles.

After this, Long practiced in his home town, Winnfield, and on the day that he was thirty he filed in the primary for governor. When the returns were in, it was found that he had come in third; he ran again in 1928 and won by a landslide, having conducted a campaign that set a new low in public slander, even for Louisiana (W. Adolphe Roberts has observed that had the *code duello* still been in force Long would not have been allowed to live a week), and promising new roads, bridges, schools, and free textbooks. Once in office, he proceeded to make good these promises, and though the people paid heavily for them in taxes—state taxes in Louisiana are still extremely high—they at least had, as his followers were fond of pointing out, something to show for their money. The man's personal popularity, particularly among the backwoods types to whom his appeals were primarily directed and to whom he made a point of talking in their own language, can scarcely be overestimated.

At first he had trouble with the legislature (an attempt to impeach him was defeated in 1929 by a round robin of fifteen senators), but he soon made himself master of this body, railroading bills through without debate, one after another, their purpose being usually to centralize political power in his own person. His tactics were the familiar ones of any dictator; it was as though he had borrowed something of the ideology which prevailed at this time in Italy. He surrounded himself with armed bodyguards, made a Gestapo of the state police, and even used the National Guard to conduct raids without declaring martial law. In 1930, after having prudently seen to it that a personal friend, Oscar K. Allen, would succeed him in the governor's chair, Long assumed the office of United States senator to which he had had no difficulty in getting himself elected. Through Allen, the puppet governor, he continued to dominate the state. The meetings of the legislature became an elaborate farce, and, on the frequent occasions that Huey came down from Washington to preside over them, presented a kind of comic opera which people flocked from miles around to witness: bills were adopted unread, and if a member hesitated Long would go to his desk and press the "Aye" button himself.

Long encountered his biggest resistance in New Orleans, in the form of the Old Regular organization which had elected T. Semmes Walmsley for mayor. Avowing a determination to rid the city of vice, he conducted raids with his militia upon the brothels which, since the abolition of Storyville, had reopened on the other side of Rampart Street, in the French Quarter. In 1934 Walmsley, supported by a hundred special policemen, made an effort to seize the Orleans Parish registration office but was prevented from doing so by the arrival of Long's heavily armed militia. On September 8, 1935, when he was at the height of his power and when there were startled rumors that he intended to campaign for the Presidency of the United States, Long was dramatically shot down in a corridor of the big new capitol he had erected at Baton Rouge by a young man whose father-in-law, a judge, had been slated for removal by the Long machine. Long was forty-two when he died, and it is probable that no other figure in American politics has ever achieved such prominence in so short a time. His career provided the subject for a number of contemporary novels, of which Robert Penn Warren's *All the King's Men* is easily the best known.

Such was Long's popularity in Louisiana that his machine lasted another five years in spite of the fact that the men in whose hands he left it were both weak and corrupt. Allen died in office, and the administration of Richard W. Leche, who resigned in 1939, was so scandalous that the Federal Government intervened and secured the conviction of a number of high-ranking officials, including President James Monroe Smith of Louisiana State University. Even after Leche's resignation the machine continued to function under the direction of Huey's brother, Earl, who had been lieutenant-governor and now served as governor until 1940, when a reform party succeeded in electing Sam Jones. Reform parties, however, have never proved very popular in Louisiana, and at this writing Earl Long is once more back in the saddle—his brother's ghost, as it is said locally, having presided at the polls. There is still magic in the name, and Louisiana abounds in the tangible benefits which its tyrant conferred upon it: toll-free bridges, improved highways, free textbooks for the public schools, a seven-mile seawall along the New Orleans lakefront, New Orleans Airport (which when it was built was the largest and most modern in the world), the Huey P. Long Bridge across the Mississippi, the magnificent capitol at Baton Rouge, a greatly enlarged Charity Hospital, and above all the Louisiana State University, which was Huey Long's particular pet, upon which he lavished enormous sums, saying he wanted to provide the youth of the state with the opportunities which he himself had lacked as a young man.

[8]

During World War II New Orleans was flooded with migrants: the shipyards and the big industrial plants employed many thousands of workers of both sexes, and for several months there was a serious housing shortage. Public facilities, especially transportational, were severely taxed, and long lines waited outside the restaurants. Many of these workers stayed on after the war, creating a housing problem which could only be solved by increased suburban development: Metairie, Gentilly, the lakeside area, and the Jefferson Highway as far west as Harahan began to be built up solidly, and shopping centers with mammoth supermarkets began to make their appearance. Motels, many of them equipped with swimming pools, cropped up by the score along the Airline and Gentilly highways, pushing the rural boundaries back still farther; a few of the more luxurious ones, like the De Ville, the Capri, and the Pan American, even settled right in the heart of the city. Industries, particularly petroleum and metal, have continued to expand steadily, and New Orleans now produces more aluminum than did the entire nation before World War II.

Although the biggest physical changes in New Orleans have occurred in its periphery, the center of the city has also altered considerably. A number of large apartment houses have appeared on the edge of the business district, automobile traffic has been accelerated by an ingenious system of over- and underpasses, a single railroad station unites several major lines which formerly maintained separate terminals, a branch of the Louisiana State University has been established on the lakefront, and the newly opened Mississippi River Bridge now joins New Orleans directly to Algiers. But the biggest building development has been at the western extremity of the business district, in the vicinity of Poydras Street and Loyola Avenue, where a former Negro slum is being replaced by a gigantic new Civic Center, which, when completed, will be the center of a landscaped park area extending all the way from the new Union Terminal to the Municipal Auditorium across Canal Street. Most of these buildings are finished, and the City Hall has already moved from its ante-bellum home on St. Charles to the spacious new headquarters.

Concurrent with these changes have come others which are not so welcome, such as a phenomenal rise, early in 1958, of the city's crime rate. The genial administration of its popular mayor, deLesseps Morrison, has not proved as productive of reform as his supporters in the last election might have wished: there have been a few shake-ups, notably in the Police Department, but these and other reforms have been accomplished by an independently organized citizens' investigating committee which has not always enjoyed the mayor's blessing. A tradition of corruption is so firmly established in the local politics that it can scarcely be expected to disappear overnight: one consoles oneself by saying that conditions generally are better than they were; that much at least is true, even of the Morrison administration.

THREE

Neighborhoods

The French Quarter

THERE is a certain unreality about the French Quarter, as there is about Venice: it has the quality of a permanent illusion. This, as in the case of the Italian city, has something to do with the extravagance of the architecture (so unlike any other in the United States) and something also to do with the peculiarly luminous quality of the light in New Orleans, and with the river mists that tend to overhang this part of the city, giving a mysterious and mirage-like appearance to its buildings. The French Quarter is like a dream, a dream framed by a fig tree—by such a tree, for instance, as grows, or used to grow, in the courtyard of the old Café Lafitte on Bourbon and St. Philip.

Not that vitality is lacking, especially in the upper reaches of Bourbon Street, which is loud with honky-tonks and crowded with visitors from all over the country, not to mention servicemen and country boys gawking at strip-tease acts through doors left wide open for just that purpose, as advertisements, while barkers exhort them to enter ("No cover charge, no minimum, beer thirty-five cents a bottle"). The first six or eight blocks of Bourbon Street are a regular Circus Maximus, at least in the evening: in the mornings and afternoons this section has a faded, tired look, like that of a street-walker before the first strains of Dixieland jazz, about nine in the evening, cause her to put on her make-up, swallow a straight slug of whisky, and saunter forth on the street in a low-cut dress and impossibly high heels. Yet Bourbon Street, for all its swirling nocturnal life, seems also curiously unreal and to partake of the general quality of illusion.

The whole neighborhood, of course, is a shell—a shell which has been inhabited by so many lives that those of the moment seem only of a relative and temporal consequence. It is rare that one feels this in an American city; it is a common enough experience in London or Paris or Rome, but one is not prepared for it here. And the natural restlessness of American life exaggerates it: whereas, say, a restaurant in London may never have been anything except a restaurant, or a private dwelling anything but a private dwelling, these buildings have been used for so many different purposes (as restaurants, as private homes, as saloons, as laundries, as brothels, as factories, as banks, as night clubs, as grocery stores, as warehouses, as antique shops) that they have ceased to have any identity except a purely physical one, and this too has in many cases been seriously altered.

It is essentially a transient neighborhood, a neighborhood of apartment and rooming houses. The buildings are old, but no one seems to have grown old in them, or along with them, and this results in a lack of rapport between the houses and their occupants; it is the relationship one has with a hotel rather than with a home, with an acquaintance rather than with a friend or lover. It is all a long, one-night stand. There is a certain melancholy in this, and the French Quarter, in spite of its surface gaiety, is not really a happy place.

Then there is sex. In no other neighborhood anywhere in the world, so far as I know, is the importance of sexual desire acknowledged so universally, nor its presence felt so profoundly—not even in places dedicated almost exclusively to its satisfaction, like the notorious Barrio Chino in Barcelona or the San Paoli district in Hamburg. There it is a mechanical thing, rather like the endless capping of bottles in a brewery display window, but here it is organic and invades every area of human consciousness and activity. If there is any justice in the by-now classic comparison of desire to a streetcar, this is certainly the most crowded streetcar in town—one which everyone rides and from which, at least in the Quarter, few ever seem to descend or wish to descend.

Sex in the Quarter is not specialized: it is all-pervading. It was not always like this, however. Before the last remnant of the Tenderloin, or red-light district, was destroyed in the thirties, there were three streets in the Quarter proper (Dauphine, Burgundy, and Rampart) where prostitutes entertained their callers quite openly, with very little interference from the police. One could walk the entire length of Royal or Chartres Street without encountering a single street-walker or meeting with any of the more public manifestations of

desire. Now all this has changed. Sex has gone underground, with
the paradoxical result that it is more in evidence than ever. The prostitutes have dispersed, not only throughout the Quarter but throughout
the entire city, and of course the number of streetwalkers has vastly
increased. But perhaps the biggest change has been in the public itself: many of the ordinary people one passes in the streets of the
French Quarter today seem to have one thing on their minds, and
one thing only. It is usually a matter of glances, overt or covert as
the case may be: one feels oneself looked at, appraised, and either dis-
missed or accepted. If one is accepted, there is a slackening of pace, a
backward glance, a pause in front of a shop window, and, if one is
sufficiently interested to follow up these invitations, a conversation
which seals the meeting one way or another. Casual pickups of this
type, the basis of which is usually noncommercial, are everyday
events in the lives of a large proportion of French Quarter inhabitants.
The individuals involved rarely repeat the experience more than
once or perhaps twice with the same person, thereby avoiding any
emotional (or legal) complications, as well as the feeling of re-
sponsibility which attaches to a more permanent relationship. It is
an utterly promiscuous, utterly pagan way of life. Probably it is
shocking, but no one appears to be seriously shocked—which, perhaps, is most shocking of all.

Every conceivable type of sexual relationship is represented by the
people who walk the streets of this neighborhood. Of the more ordinary perversions, homosexuality is of course the most evident, and it is
scarcely an exaggeration to say that the number of male streetwalkers exceeds that of the female. There are at least a dozen bars in
the Quarter frequented almost exclusively by inverts of both sexes,
while on the edge of town, just across the city line in Jefferson Parish,
a prosperous night club retains a whole army of female impersonators
who practice prostitution on the side—and sometimes on the premises.
Certain movie houses both in and out of the Quarter are known meeting places for homosexuals, and most of the brothels employ at least
one male prostitute.

The atmosphere of sexuality which overhangs the whole French
Quarter is heaviest in the bars. They are unlike the bars of any other
city: they have a secretive, even a slightly sinister, quality, and they
are usually so dark that, as in a movie, you must wait a few moments
before your eyes can make the necessary adjustment. When they
have done so, the first thing they encounter is other eyes: in the

Quarter bars, everyone watches everyone else with an intensity that one would be justified in resenting anywhere else; here it is a tradition, and in any case it is probably more curious, perhaps even more ludicrous, than it is annoying. There is very little conversation, and that usually in whispers. The sinister appearance of these places is not infrequently justified by what goes on in them: they are focal points for all manner of crime, petty and otherwise. Patrons have been stabbed and shot to death in them (when this happens too often, as in the case of the Salle d'Armes on Conti and Exchange Alley, the police sometimes close them permanently); given lethal doses of knockout drops; and robbed in a variety of ingenious ways by B-girls and by hoodlums posing as customers. They are the rendezvous of dope vendors, stick-up men, and racketeers of every description. Occasionally the bars themselves are held up: when this happens, the newspapers make much of it, and the more law-abiding citizens, particularly those who live uptown, feel oddly gratified. From time to time they are raided (there is a drive on at the moment), but these raids usually coincide with a political campaign of one sort or another and have nothing loftier for their purpose than the securing of votes; they have no permanent effect upon the places involved. At the time they occur, however, they cause considerable excitement: whispers that the "heat is on" fly up and down Bourbon Street, friends telephone one another, the news comes out in the papers, which have a cruel habit of printing the names and addresses of everybody who has been taken to the police station for patronizing a "questionable establishment" (they are seldom detained for more than an hour or so), and there is a general flurry of consternation and dismay.

All this is certainly very depressing, and it is true that the spectacle of human desire on such a level and on such a scale adds to the general melancholy of the place, but of course there is more to the French Quarter than that. Not everyone who visits here will want to enter the bars, and it is possible for virtue, if it is secure, to survive a stroll on Bourbon Street. The architectural beauty of this part of town, even if you have not been prepared for it in advance by innumerable photographs, can be breathtaking. The best time to see it is in the late afternoon, preferably after a light shower, when the faded pink, ochre, and (loveliest of all) the natural brick exteriors are incandescent with the kind of light which one sees only after rainfall, and the foliage in the courtyards is still wet and glistening. (This is true of every street except upper Bourbon, which has a tawdry look by

A VIEUX CARRE COURTYARD

EIGHTEENTH CENTURY COTTAGE, VIEUX CARRE

daylight.) And of course you must explore the place on foot, for you cannot really take in very much from the window of a car, besides which the motorist behind you is certain to be in a hurry: these narrow one-way streets must accommodate an unusually heavy volume of traffic. Anyway, what is most beautiful in the Quarter is not what you see immediately; the excitement of wandering about these streets is partly a matter of discovering the various angles from which, at your leisure, you can admire the houses and the courtyards. And there are delightful surprises in store for you: narrowly avoiding a giant ashcan set squarely on the sidewalk of a particularly disreputable-looking alley, you may suddenly glimpse, through the grille of a massive iron gate, a patio more beautiful than you have seen anywhere else in New Orleans—a miniature paradise sparkling with flowers, shaded by fig and banana trees, and murmurous with the sound of water plashing in a fountain.

It is a neighborhood of contrasts. There are some real slums (along Burgundy Street, for instance, and between Chartres and Decatur in the vicinity of the French Market) and they are adjacent to, and backed up against, some of the finest dwellings in the Quarter, with the result that property values have become terribly confused: homestead appraisers have a hard time of it in this part of town. The situation is further complicated by the presence of Negro dwellers—a circumstance which is certain to lower the value of real estate in any Southern city, though probably less so here than in any other. The Negroes in the Quarter get along pretty well with their white neighbors, on the whole, and if they are aware that the latter resent their presence they are careful not to show it nor to return the resentment, at least publicly. The whites, for their part, have behaved with a decorum that distinguishes them from the white residents of mixed neighborhoods in other cities: there has never been any window smashing or vandalism for this reason in the French Quarter.

In New Orleans you are always hearing people say that the French Quarter, while it might be interesting and convenient as a place to live, is no place in which to bring up children. Perhaps this is one reason why one sees so few children here, particularly white children, and I suppose that the slums, the night life, and the excessive sexuality of the place are sufficient to account for this feeling: certainly you would expect a child brought up in such surroundings to differ markedly from other children; and though some would be sure to survive the experience morally (there *are* a few nice people who were born in the Quarter and who still live here), I should imagine that a parent would be justified in thinking twice before taking the chance, particularly with the problem of juvenile delinquency what it is in the city. The toughness you note on the gamin-like faces of the youth of this neighborhood is real, not assumed: no need to play cowboy here, and illusions melted in the cradle. Actually crime is no more common here than in other sections of the city; there is more housebreaking uptown, where the streets are more poorly lighted and where the large, dark yards afford ideal protection for miscreants. In the French Quarter it is not so much the violation of morality as the absence of it which is disturbing: one has the impression of existing in an atmosphere from which it has been excluded *naturally*, as if because of the humidity.

The white people you see in the Quarter are of three classes: the natives, out-of-towners who have settled here more or less permanently, and transients who stay anywhere from a weekend to a couple of months. The natives are a rather hard-looking lot; the men are mostly laborers and skilled workmen, and live with their families in little Victorian houses of the shotgun variety—half a dozen people crowded into half a duplex. On a summer evening, when the front door is left open for coolness, you can see them all watching TV in the living room, which is invariably the one facing the street, or sitting on their steps (these houses seldom have front yards or porches). It is one of the many paradoxes of this neighborhood that the people who have lived in it longest live in the newer houses (a Victorian house is considered new in the Quarter), while the older dwellings are nearly all owned or rented by out-of-towners. These natives are a hybrid group: the basic mixture of French and Spanish has been complicated by many other strains, the commonest of which are African and Indian, so that they are swarthy almost without exception. Though intimate enough with one another, they maintain an aloofness toward the other two classes that is marvelously absolute. Perhaps, being outnumbered and lower placed economically, they feel somewhat defensive; at any rate, they have succeeded in cultivating an indifference which, if it has not yet become quite sincere, is certainly group acting of the very highest order. These people look through you as if you did not exist: by not so much as the flicker of an eyelash will one of them, seated on his cypress door-stoop, acknowledge the fact that you are passing within two feet of him on the sidewalk. It is rather disconcerting—particularly since the latter-day tradition in the Quarter is to stare.

The second class, composed of settlers from out of town, usually Northerners, is the most numerous. It is they who set the pace of life in the neighborhood and who define its atmosphere; it is they, too, who have kept up the old buildings. They are the real lovers of the French Quarter; the natives never really see it. They are converts, and the zeal of converts is legendary. They came here once as tourists, fell in love with the place, and stayed on—or went home only long enough to settle their affairs before returning. They bought the old houses, restored them more or less amateurishly, depending upon their taste and means, and settled down in them. Though fairly prosperous as a class, it was a common experience for them to under-estimate the cost of restoration, which is prodigious, and to borrow from homestead associations, thus creating another tie besides the emotional one. Few of them could afford, after this outlay, to live alone in the bigger houses, so they found it necessary to divide them up into apartments; this cost still more money, but it looked like a good investment in the long run, and of course landlordism created additional ties.

Usually these people, after spending so much time, energy, and money on their homes, are quite understandably reluctant to sell them, but a few of those in whom the sense of attachment is less than the sense of enterprise have realized considerable profit by doing this sort of thing over and over. There is still money to be made here in this way, though it takes rather more shrewdness than is possessed by most of the people who fall in love with the Quarter; on the whole, it is much easier to lose a fortune restoring the old mansions than it is to make one. A few have invested their money (with no great hope of multiplying it sensationally) in small businesses—tearooms, gift shops, and the like—which they operate in the pleasantly lackadaisical manner that characterizes most commercial activity in the Quarter.

Most of the social life in the neighborhood revolves about this class, which naturally contains many cliques, some of them mutually exclusive. There is frequent entertaining, and there are all sorts of clubs, such as the Patio Planters, who meet once a month in one another's gardens to discuss matters relating to the local flora and architecture; the Louisiana Historical Society, which holds its meetings in the Cabildo; Gallery Circle, a theatrical organization; and many others. And of all the people in the city, these are the most patriotic. New Orleans is not famous for its civic-mindedness, but this class furnishes most of what there is here of it: they are the petition framers and the petition signers, the writers of letters to the mayor and to the newspapers, the most articulate and the most intelligent defenders of the French Quarter against attacks on it from the outside—particularly from the Garden District, whose inhabitants have a tendency to regard the whole area with fastidious aversion as one great slum.

At its lowest level, this class includes a set of rather raffish bohemians of the type one used to see in Greenwich Village, in Taos, in Provincetown, and in Woodstock (New York), a set composed of painters who do not paint, writers who do not write, and composers who do not compose. What they like to do is talk, and of course drink, and above all else they like to argue: any subject will serve as a pretext, and when they argue they will gesture violently as they imagine is done on the Left Bank, unaware that this sort of thing went out of fashion in Paris at least a quarter of a century ago. Some of them are still reading Freud, or at least about Freud; a few attempt Sartre in the paper-back translations or make a stab at Dr. Suzuki on Zen Buddhism; others, less conscientious, have not advanced beyond the writings of Allen Ginsberg and Jack Kerouac, whose *On the Road* has become a sort of Bible for all these people (New Orleans being, together with San Francisco, one of the centers of the new Beat Movement); and of course there is the usual quota of Yogi and bongo drum enthusiasts. Most numerous of all are the progressive jazzers, who congregate nightly at Papa Joe's, on Bourbon, which has what is regarded as an "enlightened" juke-box and is perhaps the smallest bar in the whole French Quarter.

The painters are the most abundant, and perhaps it is unfair to say of them that they do not work, for when the weather is good Pirate's Alley is full of them and of their efforts—water-color views of the neighborhood, mostly, turned out with the ease of a Woolworth employee wrapping packages, and sold to the tourists for anywhere from two to ten dollars apiece. (The lack of really serious art in the French Quarter has always been something of a mystery.) This element is on the increase; you see it everywhere now, particularly in the vicinity of Jackson Square, and, except for their beards, it is sometimes hard to distinguish the men from the women, especially at a distance, for they dress identically. As a rule they are harmless enough: a certain amount of brawling is to be expected among them, but it takes place usually in their own apartments (this is a tenant class exclusively, and On the Road), disturbing no one but the landlord and the other occupants of the building. Wife swapping is fairly common among the minority who are married. How they exist (particularly the poets and the composers, for whom the opportunity of commercializing their talents is not so immediate) is a subject for endless speculation: a few of them undoubtedly have private means; others, the black sheep of solid Midwestern or New England families, depend upon checks from home—bribes, in some cases, to keep them at a safe distance.

The third class, who are the transients and tourists, though numerically smaller than either of the other two, is the one which is probably most in evidence. Royal Street, the main shopping thoroughfare of the Quarter, is full of them by day, and Bourbon by night. The more affluent among them stop (when they choose to stay in the Quarter) at the Monteleone, at the Lafitte Guest House, or at the Maison de Ville; those with less money to spend rent rooms and apartments by the day or week at places like the Cornstalk House, Tom Sawyer's Lodge, and the Opera House Hotel. They pour into the antique shops, overflow the restaurants, and invade the courtyards, photographing everything in sight; and of course nearly everyone is glad to see them, for they bring money into the city: if it were not for them, places like Antoine's and Galatoire's would simply go out of business—and the natives like to eat there too every now and then. On such occasions as the Sugar Bowl game on New Year's Day, Mardi Gras, and the Spring Fiesta it is impossible to get any sort of accommodation in the downtown area without advance reservations; it is difficult enough even on an ordinary weekend.

But not all the visitors to New Orleans are prosperous. Vagrants from all over the United States flock here, especially in the winter; it is a little like Miami that way, only New Orleans attracts a more indigent class since the cost of living here is lower and does not fluctuate from winter to summer. New Orleans is the only city of any size in the United States where a telephone call costs only a nickel and where for seven cents you can ride a streetcar or a bus anywhere in town: it is a hobo heaven. The Quarter is full of bums and wineheads; their favorite hangout is the corner of Exchange Alley and Iberville. Some of them sleep in the dormitory of the Baptist Mission on Bourbon and Esplanade, but this fills up early and besides they must be in by ten o'clock, which is a little inconvenient, and in the early morning hours you will find them everywhere—in the doorways of dark alleys, on benches in Jackson Square, and in freight cars down by the docks. There are so many of them that the police simply don't bother; after all, there is a limit to the number that the jails can accommodate.

Besides the hobos and wineheads there is another type of vagrant which is becoming increasingly common in the Quarter, and that is the male prostitute. The pickings here have always been good for these youths, particularly during the Mardi Gras season, when the town is flooded with free spenders in search of thrills; and because of the tolerance with which they are treated by the police and the inhabitants of the neighborhood, the French Quarter has become a sort of national capital for this particular brand of vice. After dark the hustlers are thick as flies in and around Jackson Square, and of course Bourbon Street is overrun with them, wearing their uniforms of tight-fitting Levi's and T-shirts. Not all of them are professionals. Seamen who have jumped ship or who are awaiting assignments sometimes choose this way of life as a temporary expedient, as do also youths from out of town who are looking for legitimate employment and have not yet succeeded in finding it: the recent unemployment, caused by economic recession, naturally increased the number of these. There is still a third group, the weekend hustlers, composed of youths from the country, servicemen from various nearby posts, and sometimes even of college students, who come to the French Quarter for a good time and choose this way of financing their excursions.

Geographically, the French Quarter consists of the area bounded by the river and Rampart Street and by Canal and Esplanade. It is a fairly clean-cut rectangle, whence the name *Vieux Carré* (Old Square). The principal thoroughfares, running from Canal to Esplanade, are Decatur (originally the Rue de la Levée), Chartres (the lower part of which, from the Cathedral to Esplanade, was formerly known as the Rue de Condé), Bourbon (originally the Rue de Conti), Dauphine (originally the Rue de Vendôme), Burgundy, and Rampart. Decatur Street, which runs along the docks, has a strong maritime flavor. Of all streets in New Orleans, this is the one which most reminds you that you are in a seaport. There are bars for seamen and longshoremen, and they are among the toughest places in the city; there are hardware stores specializing in marine supplies; and there are clothing shops stocked with sailors' dungarees, sou'westers, rubber boots, and the like. In the vicinity of the French Market this street, particularly in the early morning hours, when the wholesalers are disposing of their produce, has the bustling vitality of an open-air market in Italy (it is very like the big one in Venice), and in fact most of the market men here are of Italian, or at least of Sicilian, origin. It is probably the smelliest street in the Quarter, what with all the fish and poultry. Chartres Street is quieter. There are a couple of bars at its upper end, but the first few blocks are mainly taken up by wholesale firms and offices of various kinds; at its center stands the cathedral, facing Jackson Square, and below this it is almost exclusively residential, all the way to Esplanade.

Royal Street was once (from about 1825 to 1850) the Park Avenue of the French Quarter, and the most pretentious houses in the neighborhood, as well as some of the most beautiful, are located on it. Now it is commercial for more than half its length, although the upper floors of the larger buildings are used for residential purposes, sometimes by the owners of the shops below—exactly as in Colonial times. (The lower floors were in many cases designed originally for business use, while the proprietor lived upstairs.) This is the street of the decorators and the antique shops—the best antique shops in America, many think, and it is fascinating to peer into their windows, particularly at night, when a green-shaded Victorian lamp throws gentle light over the satinwood and mahogany surfaces of old furniture; innumerable *objets d'art* of crystal, brass, and china, marble, ormolu and lapis; dueling pistols, rapiers, dirks, and cutlases; and heavy silk fabrics stiff with exquisite embroidery. If you are in a buying mood, you must of course beware of reproductions, which, unfortunately, are not always offered as such, and they are sometimes clever enough (particularly the European reproductions) to puzzle even the experts; there are several reproducers of antique furniture right here in the Quarter, and they do a lively business.

Bourbon Street for the first six or eight blocks is dedicated to night life; after that it becomes residential. Dauphine Street, a slum for many years, is undergoing an interesting metamorphosis, as some of the most ambitious restorations in the French Quarter have taken place here in the past few years: one of them, undertaken by an enterprising New Orleans businessman, has recently been sold by him to a wealthy out-of-towner for a small fortune; among its features is a swimming pool—the first (though not the last, as others have been installed since then) in the French Quarter. Dauphine is mostly residential, and, for the first few blocks, is still partly colored, though the Negroes are slowly but surely being pushed out as the houses change hands: the new owners, anxious to raise the value of their property, show an increasing tendency to rent only to whites. The same thing is happening on Burgundy Street, though there the Negroes are more firmly entrenched; lower Burgundy is mixed, but its upper blocks are exclusively colored. Rampart Street, the western boundary of the Quarter, is chiefly commercial—automobile dealers, parking lots, bars, and restaurants. There are a few old dwellings on this street, but they have become disreputable rooming houses. Facing Beauregard Square (between St. Peter and St. Ann) is the big Municipal Auditorium, built in 1930.

Controversies are forever raging about which is the most beautiful house in the French Quarter, just as they are about which is the most beautiful courtyard or the most beautiful balcony. It is rather pointless, really, like trying to decide which is the most beautiful church (or fountain) in Rome: confronted with such an embarrassment of riches, it must be a rash man who can make an easy and final choice. But of course the choices do narrow down—and, if one is really familiar with the neighborhood, not always in favor of the places which have been most widely publicized. Thus, although the famous old Seignouret house at 520 Royal is praised again and again for its graceful proportions (and properly so), the house around the corner, at 720 Toulouse, about which one hears nothing at all, is just as impressive for the same reason, though in a very different way.

One of the handsomest buildings in the French Quarter, both without and within, is the old Louisiana State Bank, now an antique store, at 401 Royal; it was designed by Benjamin Latrobe, who rebuilt the national Capitol after it was burned by the British in 1813. The old Faurie mansion (now Brennan's Restaurant) has a striking façade, and, like the Seignouret house and the beautiful old Montegut mansion at 731 Royal, which dates from 1795, is one of the best examples in the city of the type of dwelling favored by the wealthier colonists toward the end of the eighteenth century and the beginning of the last one.

The most pretentious houses, like the huge pile on the corner of Royal and Dumaine, now the property of Mrs. Philip Steegman, were built in the late 1830's: other striking examples are the Labranche house at 700 Royal, which, because of its sensational cast-iron balconies, is perhaps the most widely photographed residence in the

LE PRETRE MANSION, VIEUX CARRE

AERIAL VIEW OF PLACE D'ARMES, VIEUX CARRE

neighborhood; and the towering Le Prêtre mansion at 716 Dauphine, a mysteriously beautiful building of unique proportions, now in a sad state of dilapidation. Houses of this type continued to be built right on up to the Civil War: Matilda Gray's massive residence at 704 Esplanade was constructed in 1856.

In contrast to these, the very earliest houses in the French Quarter, even the most elegant ones, are characterized by a simplicity, even a severity, of line: the difference between the Merrieult house at 529 Royal (1792) and the Labranche house is the difference between an eighteenth and a nineteenth century aesthetic. The oldest building in New Orleans—perhaps in the entire Mississippi Valley—is Madame John's Legacy (about 1730) at 632 Dumaine, a curious structure of the raised cottage type, the ground floor being of brick and the upper of cypress. Other interesting eighteenth century cottages are the Café Lafitte at 941 Bourbon, popularly supposed to have been a blacksmith shop belonging to Jean and Pierre Lafitte, and the recently restored house at 625 Dauphine, adjacent to the old Debois mansion. The Ursuline Convent, at 1114 Chartres, perhaps the second oldest building in the city (1749), is exactly like any eighteenth century institutional structure in France; there is absolutely nothing about it that suggests a Colonial influence—even the little formal garden in the front yard, with its beds arranged in strict geometric patterns, reminds one of Versailles and Fontainebleau.

The buildings around Jackson Square have considerable architectural interest, and the whole square has a symmetry lacking in most American parks: it has something of the atmosphere of Gramercy Park in New York, though it would not be easy to say quite why—certainly the arrangement of buildings and their function are very different. Even in Europe you seldom see a *place* as neatly balanced as this one, with the cathedral and the twin buildings, the Cabildo and the Presbytère, on either side, facing the river; and with those other twins, the Pontalba Buildings, their massiveness relieved by lacy cast-iron balconies, facing each other on the north and south sides of the square. The only feature tending to spoil the symmetry of the scene is the cupola on the Cabildo, which is not duplicated on the Presbytère. In the exact center of the park stands an equestrian statue of Andrew Jackson, on the base of which General Butler, with typical truculence, ordered the following inscription carved: "The Union Must and Shall Be Preserved."

Aside from such monuments as these, there are three public buildings of interest in the French Quarter: the old United States Mint, a box-like, severely neoclassic structure set rather too close to the street for proper appreciation of its dimensions (it was in front of this building, now a Coast Guard supply depot, that General Butler had William Mumford hanged for tearing down a Federal flag in 1862); the Custom House (1849), an enormous, granite-faced building on Canal and Decatur whose Marble Hall, on the second floor, must rate as one of the triumphs of nineteenth century architecture in America; and the New Orleans Court Building (1910), a large but graceful edifice in the very heart of the Quarter, on Royal between Conti and St. Louis.

As for the courtyards, only a few are accessible to visitors: unless one has an entrée of some sort, he must satisfy himself with glimpses from the street through an iron gate, which can be extremely tantalizing. The ones which are open to the public are usually bait to lure customers into the gift shops which surround them or open onto them at the rear, and these have a trampled, side-show quality, complete with "wishing wells," fortune tellers, hideously painted iron ornaments, and Negro mammies, uncomfortably rigged out in the costumes of a century ago, cooking pralines on a sort of miniature stage: their minds, of course, are neither on the pralines nor on the visitors from Kansas who photograph them as avidly as if they were authentic dodoes miraculously surviving the glacial period; what they are really wondering is whether or not their children are going to get into the state university this year. Even the exquisite patio of the Seignouret house has become a hive of commercial activity, and you must visit the private houses in order to see the real thing, though there too the patios (*malgré* the Vieux Carré Commission) have often been remodeled out of all resemblance to the original—not always, it must be admitted, in poor taste, as there are numerous examples to testify, such as the yards at 926 Toulouse, at 922 St. Peter, at 1132–1134 Chartres, at 625 and 631–633 Dauphine; and at 819 Bourbon, which has a marvelous circular staircase of iron on the exterior of the slave quarter.

Seen from the street, perhaps the most beautiful courtyard in the French Quarter is that of the eighteenth century Bosque mansion at 619 Chartres: one looks through an unusually wide carriage-way (dark, as they all are) at the far end of which, at a considerable distance from the sidewalk, is a huge arch framing a fountain in the exact center of the patio. This particular patio, like a good many others, is more impressive from a distance than when you are actually standing inside it, but it has the delightful feature of connecting, by means of a low, tunnel-like passage running underneath a slave quarter, with another and still larger courtyard in the rear: taken together, the two patios extend almost to the rear of the big house on Royal, so that the entire property is nearly a block deep. Several houses in the Quarter have this arrangement: the very beautiful courtyard at 722 St. Louis is another example; here the outer court is long and extremely narrow (the width, to be exact, of the carriage entrance), with a handsome row of double galleries on one side and a very high wall on the other, while the inner patio is tiny and very nearly square, with wonderful views of the surrounding buildings. Another long, narrow court of this type, framed by an unusually graceful iron gate and having an interesting slave quarter, is located at 1215 Royal.

The double courtyard of the old Grima house, at 820 St. Louis, now the Christian Woman's Exchange, is one of the very few of those which may be freely visited and which have retained their original integrity: the smaller one, which connects the main court to the stables, is the more interesting—beautifully planted, and with an iron fountain the lower basin of which is an immense sugar cauldron. One of the smallest and loveliest patios in the French Quarter is that of Mrs. Philip Steegman at 902 Royal; its miniature quality is exaggerated by the towering walls, covered with ivy, morning glory, and bougainvillaea vines, which surround it on two sides. Architecturally, however, probably no courtyard in New Orleans is so unique as the enormous one which joins the twin buildings at 716–724 Governor Nicholls. It is much deeper than it is wide—perhaps as deep as any in the Quarter, and at its far end is a building (this is *most* unusual) which joins the other two. The ground floor of all three buildings was originally a livery stable with arches running all the way around. Many of the arches have been bricked up (the place is now an apartment house), but a few of the stalls have been left intact and are used as garages—a fact which greatly increases the value of the buildings, since garages are very rare in the neighborhood.

Where balconies are concerned, one's choice is likely to depend on whether one prefers the hand-wrought iron patterns or the later, more elaborate ones of cast iron. The former are not always simple, either, as the marvelously intricate specimens at 339 Royal, perhaps the loveliest in the entire French Quarter, will testify. Both the

Cabildo and the Presbytère have graceful wrought-iron grilles, and there are superb examples at 715 Governor Nicholls, 600 St. Peter, 617 Chartres, and 917 and 927 Toulouse. Cast iron is more in evidence, however, and is generally more sensational; having a higher carbon content it tends to rust more easily, and for that reason must be kept painted. The designs are pretty highly stylized: perhaps the two commonest are the grape, a good example of which may be seen on the beautiful old house at 720 Toulouse, and the acorn, which adorns the flamboyant balcony of the Labranche house at 700 Royal. There are handsome cast-iron brackets on the façade of the Blackshear house at 623 Bourbon; and the balconies of Matilda Gray's house at 704 Esplanade are among the most elaborately beautiful in the city. Of all the cast-iron balconies in the Quarter, however, there is none lovelier than the one at 532 Bourbon, which has an exquisitely diminutive lyre design resembling more the work of a jeweler than of an ironsmith: you would not have thought that such beauty could be achieved with so common a metal. One interesting feature of the New Orleans balconies is the *garde-de-frise*, a fan-shaped, spiked barrier, sometimes placed at either end for protection against thieves entering from adjacent balconies: a fine example is the one on the Seignouret house.

This is architecture such as you will find nowhere else in the United States, and yet in spite of the efforts of the Vieux Carré Commission, it is becoming scarcer all the time. New buildings are going up, which means that the old ones are being torn down: the process began half a century ago, when the Monteleone Hotel and the New Orleans Court Building replaced some of the loveliest houses in the French Quarter, and has continued slowly but steadily. There is now a Walgreen's on the southeast corner of Royal and Iberville; directly opposite it, on the northeast corner, an addition to the Monteleone is presently under construction; and another modern hotel is going up on the northeast corner of Royal and St. Louis on the site of the old St. Louis Hotel—it is impossible, apparently, to resist the seduction of big business.

Even sadder than the passing of the buildings, for one who has known and loved the Quarter all his life, is the disappearance, one by one, of the familiar figures one used to see in it. It was always a neighborhood of characters: there were Banjo Annie, the genial, alcoholic minstrel of the early morning sidewalks; Joseph Woodson ("Pops") Whitesell, an inspired photographer whose pictures of

New Orleans life fifty years ago are now collectors' items; Dr. I. M. Cline, a pioneer meteorologist who collected antique glassware so avidly that when he retired from the Weather Bureau (at the age of seventy-four) he was virtually obliged to open a shop on St. Peter Street; Diamond Jim Moran, whose real name was James Brocato and who was Huey Long's bodyguard before he opened a successful restaurant and had diamond fillings put in his teeth; and Biaccio Montalbano, who made a religious shrine of his delicatessen on St. Philip Street (candles and statuettes of the saints amidst a profusion of salami and assorted antipasti) and who received an apostolic benediction from Pius XI for praying in church two thousand hours for two thousand days: he also made the best and biggest sandwiches in town. Of this generation the only one who remains is Flo Field, a gifted raconteuse and anthologist of Creole humor; but a whole new crop of characters has come along: there is the Duck Girl, who may be seen at almost any hour of the day or night leading a duck through the streets by a ribbon; "Gypsy" Lou Webb, who, rigged out in a fantastic costume and a red bandanna, sits at the corner of Royal and St. Peter in all sorts of weather selling her water colors to the tourists; Mary Collins, proprietress of the Café Lafitte in Exile, with her handsome, close-cropped gray hair and sparkling blue eyes which are as innocent as they are beyond surprise; there is the witchlike little woman with a fear of elevators who moves mysteriously in and out of the Quarter restoring old houses with genius and economy, speculating in dubious antiques, and collecting lame dogs; and there is the mannish-looking newswoman on her bicycle who sells papers in all the bars and who, when crossed, has a repertory of invective and abuse that will curdle the milk in anybody's whisky punch.

The French Quarter, like any very old place, is full of ghosts—some of them quite illustrious ghosts, for a good many famous people have lived here at one time or another. John James Audubon, the artist-naturalist, had his studio at 706 Barracks and later at 505 Dauphine, and Paul Morphy, one of the greatest chess players of all time, was born at 1134 Chartres, in the same house where, thirty years later, General Beauregard was to live briefly before settling down at 934 Royal. Another native of the French Quarter was Louis Moreau Gottschalk, brilliant concert pianist and the first American composer to make use of native folk rhythms: he was strongly influenced by the slave dances which he had witnessed as a child in Congo Square, only a few steps away from his birthplace on North

Rampart. (Gottschalk was also the first American composer to be taken seriously in Europe, and he is now enjoying a revival among the hi-fi fans; a number of his albums have recently been released on LP's.) Lafcadio Hearn, one of the most gifted of nineteenth century prose stylists, lived at 516 Bourbon before adopting Japan for his homeland; and Adelina Patti, the operatic prodigy, lived at 627 Royal. Among contemporaries, Sherwood Anderson owned the old house at 715 Governor Nicholls; William Faulkner had an apartment on the second floor of the Le Monnier mansion at 640 Royal; the late William March lived in the ancient cottage which he owned at 613–615 Dumaine; and Tennessee Williams occupied the second-floor apartment at 632 St. Peter.

And so the French Quarter has reality after all. The ghosts are a fact, the Duck Girl is a fact, the buildings are a fact, Bourbon Street is a fact. They can all be proved to exist, yet it is extraordinary how, when you are in this part of town, you seem to be moving about in a kind of elaborate dream; and how, when you are outside it, you remember it precisely as you recollect a dream—in apparently unrelated fragments, dimly in parts and in other parts more vividly than you would recall events in your workaday life. And returning to the place will not change any of that: you return only to renew the illusion, as one will sometimes continue to have the same dream again and again. When you come back, the dream will be waiting for you, framed by a fig tree. If you stay away long enough, of course, it will fade; even the sharpest details will become blurred, and finally it will recede altogether. Only the tree will be left.

The Garden District

It is a charming name for any neighborhood—and, in this case, accurate as well, though the accuracy may be accidental, for there is a theory that the name derives from the truck farms which occupied this part of the city before the wealthier American families began to build on it in the 1830's.

Today there is something rather sad about these gigantic ante-bellum mansions set in their vast lawns: they have a haunted look, and even the ones which have been kept up seem to belong to the past rather than to the present, and to partake of the quality of illusion that pervades the neighborhood. Perhaps it is because these houses look today exactly as they looked a hundred years ago that they seem slightly unreal—the life that is lived in them now is not the same, for better or for worse, and can never be again. It may have been pleasant to own a house with thirty rooms when labor, including slave labor, was cheap and abundant, but today it is more painful than pleasant, and the families who can afford such luxury are few and far between. This part of the city is like an elegant corpse: the polish of the surface only serves to emphasize the decay which is inner and essential. It has been well preserved, but it is still a corpse.

Oddly enough, you do not feel this way about the French Quarter, which of course is much older. The French Quarter has reality, though its reality is a tawdry one. It is alive, and it is alive because it has had so many lives: each time it has begun a new existence it has had to forget the old one. But the Garden District has had only one life, and it has not forgotten it. It was one of the last refuges of ante-bellum aristocracy in the South, perhaps the very last, and the memories linger on—memories of an easy, gracious, and luxurious way of life possible to a privileged few in a society as autocratic as any which ever existed on this earth.

Aristocratic associations were present from the first: this land belonged originally to Pierre Philippe de Marigny, biggest landowner in New Orleans in the late 1770's and host to the future King of France when Louis Philippe, then the Duc d'Orléans, visited the city in 1798 with his brothers, the Duc de Montpensier and the Comte de Beaujolais. De Marigny's daughter married a Livaudais (the Livaudais family, still very active in civic and social affairs, was one of the first in Louisiana), and in time the land became part of the sugar plantation of François Livaudais. In the spring floods of 1816, the Mississippi broke its bank near what is now Carrollton Avenue and inundated the area for miles around: Mr. Livaudais's mansion, still unfinished, was ruined, as was also his sugar crop. But the incident proved to be a blessing, for as a result of it the ground was raised several feet by alluvial sediment; the land thus formed was not only high and dry but unusually fertile as well. Mr. Livaudais never rebuilt on it, however, and, though he remained in possession of the land, it became a truck-gardening and Negro residential zone. (There is still, after all these years, a little island of Negroes in the Garden District, at Camp and Eighth streets.)

After the Louisiana Purchase, New Orleans began to fill up with Americans: by 1820 they outnumbered the Creoles, who despised them, three to one. The period from 1830 to 1860 was the most prosperous in the city's history; the newcomers were ambitious and aggressive, and they became rich almost overnight. In the 1830's a group of them approached Mr. Livaudais with an offer to purchase the area bounded by what is now Jackson and Louisiana avenues and Magazine Street and St. Charles Avenue; he accepted, whereupon the village of Lafayette was created. As time went on and the distance separating this village from the city proper began to be built up, it became a legitimate section of New Orleans—the American section.

An intense rivalry existed from the first between the Creole and American elements, and it was in this spirit of rivalry, and at this time of unparalleled prosperity on the part of the American population, that the Garden District was built up. The Creoles, proud of their French Quarter mansions, had always scoffed at the homes of the Americans, whom they regarded as little better than barbarians

—and it is true that, culturally, the American population at that time compared unfavorably with the Creole. Now the tables were to be turned, architecturally at any rate: no money was spared, and the result is a neighborhood which, like the French Quarter, though for different reasons, is without equal in this country.

These houses are overwhelming. To say that they are usually two stories high with an attic, which is true, does not convey a proper sense of their height, for the ceilings are so lofty (eighteen feet in some cases) that a single story in ante-bellum times was easily the equivalent of two stories nowadays. And to say that they often contain as many as thirty rooms, which is also true, is misleading again, for the floor area of these rooms is enormous. The early nineteenth century architects were shrewd: they knew that high ceilings, transoms, and floor-to-ceiling windows made for coolness, and of course coolness, with the New Orleans climate what it is in midsummer, was a must. They built almost exclusively in the neoclassic manner: there is the inevitable Greek portico at the front of the house—or rather a pair of porticoes, one for each floor—with a pediment on top. The first floor was sometimes raised several feet off the ground, so that there was a basement as well as an attic, making the building still higher. Naturally they took a long time to build: slave labor was used at first, but as the price of slaves became increasingly higher, it was often cheaper to hire free Negro workmen or Irish immigrants, the first boatload of whom arrived here in the 1840's. The Irish settled just across Magazine Street in an area which came to be known as the Irish Channel. It is one of the toughest neighborhoods in town, though it is adjacent to the most select: on a hot summer night, when the leaded glass windows of the mansions are left open, the sound of juke-boxes in the Magazine Street dives violates the decorum of many a genteel parlor.

It was really extraordinary, all this neoclassicism in the Deep South in the middle of the nineteenth century. In New Orleans the fever mounted to such a pitch that plans were formed for the creation of a Greek center at what is now Coliseum Square, just outside the Garden District proper. There was to be a university or *Prytanium* (hence the street name *Prytania*), an Olympic stadium, and a forum for public meetings. Many street names were changed at this time: Plaquemines Street (so called because of the row of persimmon trees with which it was lined) became Coliseum, and a whole row of streets was named after the nine muses. The project was finally abandoned, and the only reminders of it nowadays are the street names and the architecture.

Houses of this type are common enough throughout the Delta—they are especially numerous at Natchez—but the Garden District architects added certain features borrowed from the Creoles, like the ornamental ironwork on the railings of the galleries and on the fences surrounding the yards. Some of these architects were men of genius, like the elder James Gallier, who designed the old City Hall, the Boston Club, the Pontalba Buildings, and the first St. Charles Hotel. An Irishman of eclectic taste, widely traveled in Europe and America, Gallier had studied in the art schools of Dublin and London before emigrating to this country. He was drowned off Cape Hatteras in 1866 when a hurricane sank the *Evening Star*, the vessel on which he was returning to New Orleans from Europe by way of New York. His son, James Gallier, Junior, was also a distinguished architect—he is remembered as the builder of the old French Opera House, which was nationally famous for its acoustics. Two other gifted architects left their mark on the neighborhood: James Freret, member of a prominent New Orleans family (there is a street here named after them) who studied in Paris at the Beaux Arts; and Henry Howard, who, like Gallier, came here from Ireland and who is known chiefly as the designer of such plantation houses as Belle Grove and Wood-lawn.

Their imitators were not always so successful. Some of the Garden District houses are merely big and vulgar, like the Nolan mansion on Coliseum. Ostentation and pretentiousness were social weaknesses of the period, and they are reflected in the architecture: today many of these houses look a little ridiculous. There was, too, a certain medievalism about the ante-bellum scene in New Orleans, a medievalism not easily excused when you compare it with other American cities in the 1850's. These houses are hard to forgive when you reflect that not until 1892, when the city numbered a quarter of a million inhabitants, was there any effort to establish a public sewerage system here; until that time, refuse was simply dumped into open gutters which, when it rained, overflowed into the street. Sanitary conditions were almost unbelievably bad, and the death rate in New Orleans was almost twice that in New York, Boston, or Philadelphia. The emphasis was all on appearances.

But on the whole the Americans accomplished their purpose, and

OLD CITY HALL (1853, JAMES GALLIER, SR., ARCH.)

GARDEN DISTRICT HOUSE (HENRY HOWARD, ARCH.)

by 1860 the Garden District had become the finest residential section in the South. It is still the most valuable property in the city, outside the commercial area, and, being subject to strict zoning laws, is almost exclusively residential. Most of the old houses are intact, and a few—but only a very few—have remained the property of the same family for a century or more, like the house at 1213 Third Street, which is still occupied by descendants of Major Andrew Hero, a Confederate officer. Others have become institutional property, like the old Cartwright Eustis home on Jackson Avenue, now Soulé College, and the house which James Freret built for Bradish Johnston at 2343 Prytania, now the Louise McGehee School for Girls. Still others have been made over into rooming houses, especially on the shabbier side of the neighborhood, where it approaches the Irish Channel—an inevitable process, not confined to the Garden District or to New Orleans. And some have been torn down entirely, like the Robb mansion, which stood on Washington Avenue and which was until a couple of years ago the Administration Building of the Baptist Theological Seminary: it too was built by Freret and decorated by Dominique Canova, nephew of the sculptor.

Once a year, in the spring, the McGehee School for Girls sponsors a public tour of some of the larger houses. It is an opportunity which you ought not to miss if you should happen to be in the city, for the interiors are well worth seeing. The things to notice are the fireplaces (marble or onyx), the carved mahogany stairs, the plaster moldings, the chandeliers and the pier-glass mirrors in their gold-leaf frames. And of course the furniture: most of it will be in dubious taste, but here and there you will see some fine Colonial pieces, like the ones from the workshops of Prudent Mallard and François Seignouret, two French cabinetmakers who came to Louisiana early in the nineteenth century.

People are forever quarreling about which is the most beautiful of these houses. For my taste, the Moran house, at 1448 Fourth, is the most satisfying of them all—it is large without being pretentious, and ornate without being vulgar. Built in 1859 by Henry Howard, it occupies, together with its grounds, almost an entire block; it is a two-story building, cement over brick, and, in spite of its size, conveys an impression of wonderful airiness and grace. The Jordan house, at 1415 Third, is perhaps the finest example of late ante-bellum architecture in New Orleans: the portico is magnificent, as is also the curved staircase indoors. There are three other mansions you should visit: the Pipes house, at 1238 Philip, with its spacious grounds; the Sarah Henderson house, by the elder Gallier, at 2221 Prytania, which has great elegance but is set rather too close to the street; and the Westfeldt house, a plantation-type building dating back to the 1820's—the oldest house in the Garden District, but not, for that reason, very typical of it.

Some of the mansions have Civil War associations, and of course these are the saddest of all, for the civilization of which this neighborhood is the product received its death stroke at Appomattox in the spring of 1865: houses continued to be built in it, but not on the same scale or in the same spirit. Jefferson Davis died in the house at 1134 First, which was built in the 1850's by J. N. Payne, whose son-in-law, Judge Charles Fenner, was a friend of Davis; and Winnie, the President's daughter, made her debut here. The Nolan mansion, at 2707 Coliseum, served as a Union headquarters during the Federal occupation, and one of the great Confederate generals, John Bell Hood, lived after his retirement at 1206 Third, now an apartment house. Hood was appointed by Davis to succeed General Joseph E. Johnston in 1864, and defended Atlanta against Sherman in one of the most important battles of the war. He died here in 1879—a victim, together with his wife and child, of yellow fever.

It is a neighborhood of ghosts, an unreal place, and the best time to see it is by moonlight, when the quality of illusion is strongest: the great houses, towering whitely out of the blackness of the yards, have a curiously theatrical look, and the whole Garden District seems like a gigantic stage set, waiting for the beginning of a performance which will give it meaning. But the waiting is in vain: this particular drama ended long ago, the principals are all dead, and nothing is left but the scenery.

The Irish Channel

Nobody knows how it got the name, but it has been called that for a very long time—ever since the 1840's, in fact, when it was first settled. There are many conjectures, one of the least fantastic of which is that the streets, owing to poor drainage, flooded every time there was a really bad rain. But there is no need for recondite explanations: the neighborhood is longer than it is wide (originally it was a single street, two blocks long) and it was inhabited by Irish longshoremen to whom nautical terms were perfectly natural and familiar.

Adele Street, which runs vertical to the river from Tchoupitoulas to St. Thomas, was the original Irish Channel, and as the neighborhood grew it lengthened as far as Laurel and widened to include the area between Josephine and Felicity: nowadays the term is used rather loosely to define the rectangle bounded by Tchoupitoulas and Magazine, and by Felicity and Jackson Avenue. For many years it was one of the most colorful parts of the city—a lusty, brawling place, not unlike certain parts of Manhattan's lower East Side. The neighborhood began to lose some of its character with the infiltration of Negroes into it early in the present century (Adele Street is now exclusively Negro), and in the thirties the whole ramshackle center of it was torn down and replaced by a huge Government housing project. The Channel never quite recovered from this blow: some of the natives settled in the new brick tenements but most of them moved away; some, reluctant to leave the neighborhood, relocated on its fringes, extending the rectangle still farther on every side except that bounded by the river.

Today it is in these fringes that you must search if you are looking for authentic fragments of the old Irish Channel. And you will not be disappointed: there will be corned beef and cabbage odors issuing from the little shotgun houses, and, in the evenings, ruddy-faced workmen in their undershirts will be taking their ease—together with their beer—on the tiny front porches. The taverns along Magazine and St. Mary will be full of roisterers, especially on a Friday or Saturday night, and a young man spoiling for a fight in one of these places will often overlook the ceremony of inviting another one to step outside: the result is apt to be a free-for-all. Quite recently, in one of the senseless drunken brawls which you can witness almost any weekend in this part of town, a man was brutally beaten to death in one of the St. Mary Street dives.

Many typically Irish customs survive here, such as the practice of "waking" the dead with an evening of revelry. Now that funerals are usually held at undertakers' parlors, the wakes are no longer so elaborate or so lengthy; formerly they lasted for as long as three days, when the odor of decomposition, in spite of camphor sprinkled liberally about the room, forced an end to the festivities. But wakes are still very much a part of the Channel tradition (Donegan's, on Jackson Avenue, is the favorite parlor), though they are more decorous than they were in the old days, when the women wailed and the men played practical jokes and nearly everyone got drunk before the night was over: the crowd was sometimes so large that strangers, attracted by the free food and liquor, were often able to crash the party—when they were discovered, a fight was sure to follow. The old Irish superstitions survive too, as you will discover if you spend much time in the neighborhood. It is considered unlucky to borrow salt or to run out of it, a sneeze at the table means that someone seated at it will die before very long, and on no account should you leave a house by any door other than the one by which you entered.

The Channel was built up by immigrants fleeing from famine conditions in mid-nineteenth-century Ireland. In New Orleans they immediately became the victims of a strong social prejudice: their living standards were low, and out of necessity they would do work which most Southerners considered beneath the dignity of white men; they thus became competitors of the Negroes, who naturally also resented them. The Irish reacted to this feeling by clanning together in the Channel and making it unsafe for strangers to visit, especially after dark.

It was not a particularly pleasant place to visit at any time: the streets were muddy, there was no sewerage and very few lights, and the whole area stank of slaughterhouses which lined the riverbank. Every family owned a few goats, which roamed the streets more or less at will. But the worst thing about the Channel was the gangs with which it was infested—the St. Mary's Market Gang, the Shot Tower Gang, the Crowbars, the Ripsaws, and several others. An interesting thing about these gangs is that they were composed not so much of thieves as of fighters: robbery, when it existed as a motive, was always secondary to battle. They fought with one another and sometimes with gangs from other parts of the city, like the Sockserhausers, a tough band of Germans from a downtown suburb.

Even policemen were afraid of the Channel in the old days—and with good reason, for more than one of them was murdered here in the line of duty, among them a Negro sergeant named Fitzpatrick. The Irish especially hated the Negroes, but no one was really safe— one morning, in St. Mary's Market, the body of a sailor was found swinging from a beef hook. Then as now, the neighborhood was full of saloons, of which the most popular were the Bucket of Blood, the Isle of Man, the Ocean Home, and the Bull's Head: all of them were equipped with free-lunch counters (an institution which is believed to have originated in New Orleans) and gave away tobacco as well. Ironically enough, the most dangerous corner in the whole Irish Channel was formed by two streets named Religious and St. Mary. St. Mary Street, where it nears Magazine, is still the toughest in the district.

The Irish Channel was not inhabited exclusively by thugs, however. There were a few law-abiding families, and they appear to have been as respected as they were respectable—as long as they were Irish. There were even a few French and German families, but no Englishman would have dared to live here. The neighborhood has produced a number of prominent citizens, including Arthur J. O'Keefe, who was mayor during the Prohibition years and who lived during the whole of his administration at 1018 St. Mary. The city's best athletes, too, have come mainly from the Channel, for sports, particularly boxing, have always been popular here—in the fifties there were boxing matches every Saturday night, and the fighters trained at the Sunny South, a combination saloon and athletic club on Tchoupitoulas near Josephine.

Today the permanent residents of Irish descent in the Channel are outnumbered or at least equaled by transients of all types—a natural development in a low-rental neighborhood with many rooming houses. The newcomers are mostly from the country, a poor-white element from the Cajun area of southwestern Louisiana, and also from eastern Texas and Mississippi. Many of them work on offshore drilling operations, and squander their wages here on liquor and women on weekends and in between jobs. The Mississippi contingent is especially numerous, and the largest of the Irish Channel honky-tonks, Mary's Tavern, now has a hillbilly band three nights a week. There is still a third element, composed of wineheads from heaven alone knows where—everywhere, it seems; certainly there are plenty of them and you come across them wherever you go, sprawled out in doorways and alleys—impervious, in the strange delirium of their world, to the flies and the hot noonday sun of this one. In this condition they are harmless enough, but when they are sober they are to be avoided, for alcohol has effaced in them any distinction between right and wrong, as it has effaced everything else: they are not really responsible for their actions and would murder you cheerfully for a bottle of muscatel or sherry. They are the latest additions to the Channel, and perhaps the most dangerous type ever to inhabit it, but fortunately they are seldom sober.

There is constant brawling among these three factions, and of course the Irish fight with all of them: it is a little as it was in the old days, when the gangs used to be at one another's throats. Gangs, for that matter, have not entirely disappeared from the Channel, only nowadays, in this age of juvenile delinquency, they are made up mostly of teen-agers. You will see them hanging around Magazine, and on St. Mary too, in their T-shirts and jeans so tight they almost appear to have been sprayed on them: during the Carnival season, when huge crowds turn out for the parades, they roam the streets in large numbers, causing no end of mischief. Until recently, a favorite hangout for these youths was the Jamaica Lounge on Magazine; it has been raided, however, and the owner threatened with loss of his liquor license for serving drinks to minors. Some of them already have impressive criminal records involving robbery and narcotics; others, at sixteen and seventeen, have become professional pimps and male prostitutes. They are as vicious a lot for their age as you will encounter anywhere—descendants, some of them, of the same young men who in 1849, instead of throwing flour at passers-by on Mardi Gras, threw quicklime and brickbats, causing so many injuries that a group of citizens petitioned the City Council to abandon Carnival altogether.

Actually, what is surprising about the Channel today is not how much it has changed, but how little. The physical change, that is, has been enormous (the place would be unrecognizable to a pre-Civil-War inhabitant) and the neighborhood has lost much of its ethnic homogeneity, but its essential character remains very much what it has always been. Traditions outlast buildings, and what has survived here is the tradition of violence. But one of the few excuses for violence (if there are any) is color, and the Irish Channel has lost much of its color. Twenty-five years ago the place was full of characters; there are still a few around, but not of the same stature— the last of them, Perfume Peggy, was laid in her grave a decade or so ago reeking of Jockey Club, her favorite scent.

Uptown

THE terms "Uptown" and "Downtown" are common to many cities: sometimes they are used rather vaguely, and there is often more than one theory concerning the areas which they are supposed to designate. This is not the case in New Orleans. Here the words have very specific meanings geographically, and they also have opposite connotations—a whole cluster of associations has become attached to them.

If you stand on Canal Street with your back to the river, Uptown lies on your left and Downtown on your right. It is as simple as that. Canal Street divides New Orleans into two parts, and almost all the neighborhoods in the city belong to one or the other of them: thus, Uptown includes the Garden District, while Downtown includes the French Quarter. At the far end of Canal Street, where it terminates in a group of cemeteries, the terms lose most of their significance and are replaced by another one, "Lakefront," which includes a large area that has been built up rather solidly in recent years.

Because the Americans settled on the south (or uptown) side of Canal Street, across from the French Quarter, the term "Uptown" came to mean not only a particular area but also a way of life, a way of life whose mores were essentially Anglo-Saxon—but not exclusively, for there were also numerous Irish and German settlers in the new neighborhood. In general, the Uptowners were blond, they were usually non-Catholic, they were enterprising with the kind of zeal which Englishmen and the descendants of Englishmen nearly always exhibit wherever they happen to settle, and they were (with the exception of the Irish laborers) fairly prosperous. They were good businessmen, and it is no accident that the city's business section grew up just south of Canal Street—first along the riverfront, and then gradually westward. Of course, the picture has changed greatly since the early days of the American domination: Uptown is inhabited by all manner of people nowadays, as is Downtown, but the connotations still persist.

Canal Street is so called because of a ditch which used to run along the southern rampart of the French Quarter. Today it is one of the widest and best-lighted principal thoroughfares in the United States, but for all its spaciousness the sidewalks overflow with pedestrians and there is fender-to-fender driving during the business hours; traffic is a problem here as in other major cities. There is something slightly suggestive of Broadway in the bustle along Canal Street, as there is also in the width of the street: no other Southern city exhibits quite so much animation. The busiest part of Canal Street lies between the river and Rampart Street, and the buildings which face on it are mostly old ones, though a few have had their façades remodeled; some even go back to pre-Civil-War times, like the Custom House and the Boston Club.

Most of the big office buildings are located in the vicinity of Canal on Camp, St. Charles, Carondelet, and Baronne streets. One of the handsomest of these is the International Trade Mart at Camp and Common, the first wholesale trading center of its kind in the country. The tallest structure in the city is still the Hibernia Bank Building at Carondelet and Gravier, with its graceful tower which rises 335 feet above the street; the light in this tower is visible from a distance of several miles in the flat countryside surrounding New Orleans—it is the first thing you see when approaching on a highway after dark. The center of the city is shifting, however, and last year the City Hall was moved from the handsome but inadequate Greek Revival building which Gallier designed in the 1850's into a modern ten-floor, eight million dollar home at Poydras Street and Loyola Avenue.

The new City Hall is to be the nucleus of a gigantic Civic Center first conceived by the late Brooke H. Duncan, a former director of the City Planning Commission. Four other large buildings, now under construction, will be grouped about it: a State Office Building ($4,000,000), a Public Library ($2,500,000), a Civil Courts Building ($2,000,000), and the Louisiana Supreme Court Building ($1,800,-000). These sites were formerly occupied by slums.

The first significant step in the westward expansion of the business area took place in 1952, when the Pan American Life Insurance Building, which many think the most beautiful in the city, was erected at 2400 Canal. Shortly thereafter a new Union Passenger Terminal was built at the corner of Loyola and Howard avenues, uniting a number of major railroad lines which had previously maintained separate stations inconveniently located at considerable distances from one another. Eventually the Civic Center will include a mile-long string of landscaped parks extending all the way from the Union Passenger Terminal to the Municipal Auditorium across Canal Street: at its center, before the main entrance to the City Hall, will be Duncan Plaza, with a large pool and fountain.

Adjacent to this project, on the west, lies the great group of buildings which comprise Charity Hospital, Veterans Administration Hospital, the Louisiana State University Medical Center, and the Tulane University Medical School. Charity Hospital, with a 3,500-bed capacity, is one of the largest in the world (a thousand babies are delivered here monthly) and one of the few hospitals in the United States which provide absolutely free care for the insolvent. It was founded in 1782 by Don Andrés Almonester y Roxas, and has been in continuous operation ever since; the present site, however, was not chosen until 1832 and most of the main buildings were constructed in 1939. The medical schools of Tulane University and Louisiana State University, which flank the hospital on either side, use it jointly as a training institution.

St. Charles Avenue (called St. Charles Street between Canal and Lee Circle) is the longest and most impressive of the uptown thoroughfares. For the first few blocks it is commercial, but above Jackson Avenue it is the most elegant residential street in the city exclusive of the Garden District, of which it is the northern boundary. There is little uniformity in the style of the houses, except in the area of the Garden District, and most of them are not really interesting architecturally, but they are nearly all big and expensive: a few have been converted into apartment and rooming houses, and others (like the aristocratic old Orleans Club at 5005 St. Charles, headquarters of a women's social and cultural organization limited to 750 members) into institutions.

Two large universities, Tulane and Loyola, are located side by side on St. Charles Avenue as it nears Carrollton. The former, with an enrollment of 6,668, was known as the University of Louisiana prior to 1883, when an endowment by Paul Tulane made possible its

PHOTO BY NEW ORLEANS CHAMBER OF COMMERCE

VIEW OF CANAL STREET ON MARDI GRAS

VIEW OF DOCKS AND PUBLIC GRAIN ELEVATOR

present site. Its 93-acre campus contains a group of rather dingy Romanesque buildings; Newcomb College, the women's division, has more attractive grounds and architecture. The Tulane stadium, where the Sugar Bowl games are held, seats 82,289 spectators. Loyola is the Catholic university of New Orleans; it was founded in 1911 by the Jesuits and has a fourteen-acre campus with red brick buildings in the Tudor-Gothic style. The dental college and the school of music are outstanding.

Part of Etienne de Boré's plantation, where sugar was first granulated, lay between St. Charles Avenue and the river, just across from Tulane and Loyola, and this land now forms a portion of Audubon Park, the second largest in the city: its 247 acres are beautifully landscaped and there is a big zoo whose features include an alligator pool, a monkey house, a tropical bird house, and a flight cage for wildfowl and water birds.

St. Charles ends at Carrollton Avenue, which is the main thoroughfare of the neighborhood of the same name. Carrollton was once a village separated from New Orleans by swamps and a few plantations; it was founded in the 1830's, and named after General William Carroll, who helped defend New Orleans against the British in 1814. In 1835 it was joined to the city by a railroad which for a time used horse-drawn cars, finally abandoning these in favor of a locomotive carrying a steam storage tank which was refilled from boilers at each end of the line; this equipment continued to be used as late as 1890, when the railroad became the property of the city public utilities service.

Carrollton still retains a slightly suburban flavor: Oak Street, where the business district is concentrated, has something of the quality of a small-town Main Street. But the neighborhood is largely residential, and rather serenely middle class—the houses are not so pretentious as those of the Garden District, but they are comfortable-looking; the yards are not so big, but they are well kept; and there are lots of trees, shrubs, and flowers.

Northwest of the Carrollton section, in Jefferson Parish, lies Metairie. Fifty years ago Metairie consisted of a few houses strung out along a gravel road; now it is almost as thickly populated as any of the better neighborhoods in the city. Metairie is full of the newly rich: the houses are big and expensive but they are not very tall (one story, mostly, and rambling all over the place in the modern manner) and the yards are even bigger than in the Garden District. These homes are air conditioned throughout, many of them have swimming pools, and you see Cadillacs, Lincoln Continentals, Jaguars and Mercedes-Benzes standing in the carports—two and sometimes three to a house. Metairie is, of course, a decorator's paradise, and there are innumerable interiors straight out of *House and Garden* that tell nothing whatever about the people who live in them.

This is the part of town where the Latin element is least in evidence, and somewhat the same relationship exists between it and the other, older parts of the city as once existed between the French Quarter and the Garden District. Indeed, Metairie is probably destined to become the Garden District of the future, for that neighborhood too was built up by *arrivistes* whose tastes were also dubious on occasion. It may take several generations, but the process is at work. Meanwhile, for those who make a religion of success and a virtue of conformity, or who have children to play in the big yards, Metairie is an ideal place to live in.

The growth of Metairie, remarkable as it has been, is less sensational than the developments which have taken place in the last few years along the Jefferson and Airline highways, also in Jefferson Parish: these are the two western arteries of the city. Jefferson Highway is built up solidly all the way to the Huey P. Long Bridge. Fifteen years ago this neighborhood had a distinctly rural atmosphere; now it is full of shopping centers supplying all the needs, real and imaginary, of its inhabitants so completely that they need never take a bus to Canal Street except in a spirit of pure adventure. It is the very essence of Suburbia—primarily a middle-class and lower-middle-class neighborhood, and very typical of what is happening today on the edges of large cities all over the nation. Its growth has been accelerated by a number of large building projects in the area, such as the construction of the Huey P. Long Bridge across the Mississippi in 1935 and more recently by the erection of Ochsner Foundation Hospital, which has already, under the direction of Dr. Alton Ochsner (a pioneer in the attempt to demonstrate a relationship between lung cancer and smoking) achieved international fame, particularly for cancer surgery: well-to-do patients come here from all over the world.

The Airline Highway, which goes out past the Airport and connects with the new causeway across Lake Pontchartrain (the world's longest bridge) is even more spectacular. During the morning and afternoon rush hours it is a little like Chicago's Outer Drive: if you get into the wrong lane you may be forced to drive for miles before you can make a turn, and there is an intricate system of overpasses and underpasses which require constant alertness. The traffic circle which connects the highway to the Pontchartrain Causeway is one of the most bewildering you have ever seen—until you have been through it several times you feel like an experimental mouse in a psychologist's maze.

Like its neighbors, the Airline is provided with shopping centers, and there is a gigantic supermarket, Schwegmann's, the second largest in a locally owned chain, where you can buy anything from chocolate-covered ants to tranquilizers—and you will need one of the latter if you go there on a Saturday afternoon. Schwegmann's is several cents cheaper on almost every item than any other store in town, which makes it popular with the masses, and the variety of its merchandise (it has one of the best liquor stores in the South, with an eclectic selection of hard-to-get vintage wines) attracts customers from all neighborhoods and in all economic brackets.

Probably the Americans never imagined, when they settled on the southwest side of Canal Street, that their neighborhood would one day extend for a distance of five miles in this direction, to lose itself at last in a string of motels between what are now the city limits and Moisant International Airport. But that is what has happened. The same thing happened to Downtown, and is happening in larger cities everywhere, where geographical factors permit. It is the triumph of Suburbia.

Downtown

THERE is nothing about Elysian Fields today that suggests heaven except its name, which seems grossly inappropriate when you contemplate the mess of railroad tracks which constitute its neutral ground down by the river, where it begins, and the squalid neighborhood which it traverses, which is lower middle class and downright slummy in spots: Blanche's disillusionment is quite understandable. However, Bernard de Marigny, the man who named it, intended it to be to New Orleans what the Champs Elysées (after which it was named) was to Paris. It was the main street of Downtown, exclusive of the French Quarter, and it is still one of the busiest.

The neighborhood which lies to the north and east of Esplanade Avenue did not come into existence until 1808, when Marigny—in order, it is said, to settle gambling debts—decided to break up his plantation, which lay just below the French Quarter: to be exact, the area bounded by the river and what is now St. Claude Avenue, and by Esplanade and Almonaster (formerly the Rue d'Enghien) avenues. This part of the city became a suburb known as the Faubourg

114

Marigny, and Elysian Fields Avenue ran through its center. It was settled by Creoles, and it was the ambition of Marigny (whose own mansion stood at Elysian Fields and the river) and other prominent French and Spanish citizens that it should surpass in magnificence the American suburb uptown; this ambition was never realized, and there was never any real competition between the Faubourg Marigny and the Garden District.

This part of town still retains its Creole characteristics—more so, in fact, than does the French Quarter, where the tourists have taken over and where many of the old houses are inhabited by people from out of town. You do not see it so much in the architecture (though there are some old buildings here) as you do in the people themselves: this is where you must search if you are looking for that nearly extinct species of citizen, the New Orleanian of Creole descent, and here he is likely to be a little more human than in the French Quarter, where the presence of so many newcomers and tourists has caused him to be suspicious and defensive; and it is the only neighborhood in town where you will still hear an occasional scrap of French—on the lips, perhaps, of a mulatto, for the results of racial mixture are very much in evidence here. The population of Downtown is hybrid generally: there was a whole colony of Germans here in the nineteenth century, whose descendants continue to live on in the neighborhood; and Italians are scattered everywhere, most thickly in the vicinity of Esplanade and the river, near the French Market.

No one knows for certain the number of New Orleanians of Italian extraction, but the figure must be prodigious. They settled all over the city and its suburbs, as well as in nearby towns (Harvey and Kenner have particularly large colonies), but they appear to be most numerous in the downtown area; they have a very active social center, Italian Union Hall, on Esplanade near Burgundy. Like Italian immigrants elsewhere in the nation, they came mostly from Sicily and Calabria, and the language which they speak among themselves, a mixture of the dialects of these regions with English, is very nearly unintelligible to a native of northern or central Italy. The Sicilian neighborhoods are easy to recognize from the cooking odors which invade the streets in the evening—the sauces are almost Orientally pungent with basil and oregano, and the ovens are full of *manicotte* and stuffed artichokes and eggplants.

Many of the Italian immigrants who settled in New Orleans came from the tiny village of Contessa Entellina, near Palermo, and, after the manner of immigrants in the free-and-easy days before restrictions were imposed, they wrote home encouraging their friends and relatives to join them, often enclosing money for that purpose. The result was a steady one-way stream of humanity between Contessa Entellina and New Orleans; that little town must virtually have been emptied of its inhabitants, while the population of this one was substantially increased. Most of the Italian stock in New Orleans has this source, and what is not generally known is that the original population of Contessa Entellina contained easily as many Albanians as Italians (it was a refugee village, one of several in Italy), which complicates the ethnical background of these people still further.

St. Joseph has always been a popular saint in Sicily, and the Italians in New Orleans have a custom of erecting altars in their homes on March 19th, St. Joseph's Day, and inviting the public to visit them, sometimes even running announcements in the Personal columns of the local papers: "Mr. and Mrs. Joseph Messina, 1236 Howard Street, cordially invite their friends and the general public to visit the St. Joseph's Altar at their residence, on March 18 and 19." These altars are often quite elaborate, with plaster statuettes and enormous candles decorated with flowers and angels, and great quantities of food are heaped upon them; when they are dismantled there is a feast for the relatives and a few specially invited guests, and what is left over is given to the poor. A bit of St. Joseph's bread, specially baked and blessed, is kept in the house to keep hunger away from it. The custom, like so many others in the city, is beginning to die out now: the younger generation tend to regard it as old-fashioned and a waste of money.

The Faubourg Marigny, which is still the heart of Downtown, received a boost in 1831, when the Pontchartrain Railroad Company built a line all the way out Elysian Fields to the lake, a distance of about five miles. This was the first railroad west of the Alleghenies; horses were used on it for the first few months, when an engine was imported from England, and in 1880 the line was acquired by the Louisville and Nashville Railroad. It continued to operate for another fifty years or so, and ran as many as seven or eight excursion trains on Sunday. The locomotive, which burned soft coal, was popularly known as "Smoky Mary," and in time the term came to apply to any train which made the run to Milneburg. Building in the downtown area was stimulated to some extent by this development, but the city grew up rather slowly in the direction of the lake because the land had to be drained before it was suitable for habitation: it is only in very recent years that the distance between the river and the lake has been built up solidly.

Esplanade Avenue, another big downtown thoroughfare, runs from the river to Bayou St. John and terminates at City Park; it is residential all the way, and, where it forms the northern boundary of the French Quarter, contains some of the biggest and finest houses on this side of Canal Street, like the mansions belonging to Matilda Gray and Germaine Cazenave Wells. Esplanade, which has a beautifully planted neutral ground (it is perhaps the shadiest street of any size in the city), has a restful and decidedly aristocratic atmosphere, and, while it is true that most of the bigger houses have been divided up into apartments, the street has somehow managed to retain an air of leisured refinement: it is what Marigny wanted Elysian Fields to be like. Just north of Esplanade, where it approaches City Park, lie the Fair Grounds, where the horse races are held for a three-month period beginning on Thanksgiving Day; the glass-enclosed, steam-heated grandstand seats six thousand, and the track is one of the best in the country.

City Park, at the end of the avenue, is the sixth largest in the United States, and there are many who think it the loveliest. Certainly it would be hard to imagine anything more beautiful than these ancient live oaks, festooned with Spanish moss, beneath which duelists in the last century settled their disputes; it was the most popular dueling spot in the city. The land at that time belonged to Louis Allard, a wealthy planter who, after disposing of it, became destitute through a series of misfortunes: he is buried beneath one of the trees of which he was so proud. The beauty of City Park lies in its trees and its lawns, which resemble certain English lawns that have been carefully tended for centuries and that, because of heavy dews and frequent rainfall, achieve a degree of lushness impossible in drier climates. At the southern end of the park is the Isaac Delgado Art Museum, a very handsome Greek Revival building which was erected in 1911 through a bequest of a New Orleans philanthropist who also endowed the Delgado Trades School, which stands nearby on City Park Avenue. Delgado was himself a lover of *objets d'art*, and his personal collection formed the center about which the museum has grown up;

the present collection, however, is merely adequate, with rather too many copies and too many portraits from the private homes of local families.

Bayou St. John, which runs alongside the entire length of the park, was once an important waterway, providing easier access to the city from Lake Pontchartrain than through the swamps which surrounded it. Toward the end of the eighteenth century, the Baron de Carondelet extended it by building a canal which enabled boats to come right up to the gates of the city: commerce flourished as a result, and a number of big plantation houses were built along the shores of the bayou. Some of these are still standing, but the oldest house on Bayou St. John antedates Carondelet's canal; it was built about 1784 and is called the Spanish Custom House because it was supposed to have been used as an official warehouse for contraband merchandise seized from pirates operating on the bayou. The shores of Bayou St. John and Lake Pontchartrain were also popular meeting places for Voodoo worshipers in the middle of the last century: Marie Laveau, queen of the cult from approximately 1830 to 1870, had her headquarters in a house which she built for herself on the lake between Bayou St. John and the little town of Milneburg, now a part of the city proper. (You can see her portrait in the Cabildo, and she is *probably* buried in the tomb which bears her name in St. Louis Cemetery Number One. You should also hear Robert Gurley's *Marie Laveau* sung by the late Oscar "Papa" Celestin to the accompaniment of his famous jazz band and recently recorded by Southland Records.)

Besides Elysian Fields and Esplanade Avenue, the two most important downtown streets are St. Claude Avenue, a continuation of North Rampart Street which crosses the Industrial Canal and, as Highway 39, goes on down the river to Arabi and Pointe à la Hache; and Gentilly Boulevard, the biggest and busiest of them all, which becomes the Chef Menteur Highway leading to the Mississippi Gulf Coast and connecting with highways to all the southeastern and northeastern states. Gentilly, the neighborhood from which the street takes its name, parallels Metairie in its development: only a few years ago it presented a decidedly rural appearance—an effect of gravel roads with a few houses and nurseries spaced out along them. Now the streets are all paved, the houses nudge their neighbors, and the nurseries, except for Farley's, seem to have disappeared. On Gentilly Road there is a big university for Negroes, Dillard, with a seventy-acre campus and impressive buildings; it was opened in 1935.

It has been claimed that the word *Gentilly* is a corruption of *Chantilly*, but a more plausible etymology is provided by John Chase in his book about the streets of New Orleans, *Frenchmen, Desire, Good Children*. All of this land once belonged to two brothers, Pierre and Mathurin Dreux, who, succumbing to the propaganda of John Law, migrated to Louisiana in the early eighteenth century. They came from the commune of Gentilly in the Department of the Seine and so gave the name to their plantation; during their lifetime here they were referred to as the Sieurs de Gentilly.

Gentilly is more bustling and less elegant than Metairie; its houses are smaller and less pretentious. It is more like the neighborhood around the Jefferson and Airline highways: there are the same shopping centers, the same drive-ins, the same mammoth super-markets. The newest and biggest of the Schwegmann stores is here, a fluorescent-lighted, air-conditioned wilderness of people pushing and pulling their supplies this way and that, very much as ants do—and of course the proportions of the building make them seem more ant-like than ever. The new Schwegmann's is a city complete in itself, with a restaurant, a bar, rest rooms, a drugstore, a barbershop, a record shop, a flower shop, and indeed almost any kind of shop you can imagine.

But the real glory of Gentilly is its motels. They line both sides of Chef Menteur Highway for miles, giving it, with their flashing neon signs, the appearance of an endless midway. They bear glamorous-sounding names (Monte Carlo, Hollywood, Monterey, Saxony) and are as expensive as the better hotels right in the heart of the city—and why shouldn't they be, what with all their services and facilities: TV in every room, air conditioning, panel ray heat, wall-to-wall carpeting, and kidney-shaped swimming pools? One of the most progressive of them, the Plantation, even has a staff of baby sitters.

Downtown, like Uptown, ends in a string of motels. Perhaps it is not quite the Champs Elysées that Marigny envisioned: the illumination is far from celestial (the preferred color, in fact, is a rather lurid shade of red), and the total effect could scarcely be termed idyllic, but then many changes have taken place in American life since 1808—including, perhaps, our notion of what is heavenly and what is not.

The River

❦ THE river is New Orleans' *raison d'être*, and it continues to be the biggest single factor in its development. The first street in the city was built along the riverfront, with its houses facing the broad yellow stream into which flow no fewer than forty tributaries from thirty-one states and Canada. A hundred miles before this august amalgam reaches its final destination it describes a crescent-shaped curve whose tips are only five miles from Lake Pontchartrain (which some geologists believe may have been formed by the Mississippi eons ago, leaving it linked with the Gulf when it changed its course), and it is between these two tips that the city has grown up.

"Weary river": the phrase is a cliché in the literature of blues songs and spirituals, and when you consider the distance the Mississippi has traveled by the time it reaches New Orleans (something like fifteen thousand miles if you include all the inland waterways) the phrase has a certain justice. It was easy, in slave days, for an analogy to suggest itself between the river and the men who sweated along its shores, and to read a symbolic meaning in its eagerness to reach the open sea after so long a journey: many slaves undoubtedly looked forward to the release which death would offer them from the cares and sorrows of an earthbound existence. The Negro, too, made a naïve identification between the Mississippi and the River Jordan: it was, like the latter, a symbol for rebirth and life everlasting.

The Mississippi is not, like many rivers, a pretty sight. Its waters are muddy and opaque, and it is too wide for you to obtain any sort of perspective that would make it appear "picturesque"; there are few natural eminences on its banks, and you would have to see it

120

from an airplane to appreciate the form and direction of it. Even from a great height it still looks yellow.

The Mississippi *looks* tired. Its waters seem the very quintessence of weariness, yet for all that it seems to be hurrying, hurrying home, back to original blue. It has a mean current, as I discovered when I was old enough to go swimming in it, for though it is half a mile wide you will have swum at least a mile by the time you reach the opposite bank: I used to know, when I set out, exactly where I would land, or rather where the current would deposit me. It is a treacherous river to navigate, too, as Mark Twain discovered; its channels are constantly shifting, and there are unexpected shallow spots right in the middle.

With the strict impartiality of nature, the Mississippi has been both kind and cruel to the city which it created: it made of it a great port, then threatened to destroy it with floods. In the early days, it was a constant struggle between the city and the river, the land and the water. Now at last the river has been tamed: it has been dredged, it has been bridged, its floodwaters have been diverted into Lake Pontchartrain, and 160,000,000 gallons of it are pumped into the city daily and purified for drinking purposes.

Before the development of railroads and the construction of the Erie Canal, the Mississippi was the sole outlet for the produce of the entire West and Middle West, and as such brought to New Orleans her greatest period of prosperity. River trade reached its peak in the 1850's, after which it declined steadily, but there is still a considerable volume of barge traffic to and from the Great Lakes; New York City, by way of the Erie Canal; and even Montreal, by way of the St. Lawrence. The year 1958, in fact, witnessed a sharp revival of barge traffic—possibly the result of economic recession, since barge rates are anywhere from one-third to one-half the rail rates. New Orleans is the terminus for some fifteen thousand miles of navigable inland waterways, and at the moment there are no fewer than seventy barge lines in active operation.

Ocean-going trade had always been handicapped by shallow water at the mouth of the Mississippi: owing to the width of the river at this point the current lost its force, and huge silt deposits had accumulated. This was a problem even in Colonial days; as early as 1721 Pauger proposed a plan for deepening the channel by means of a system of jetties, but it was never put into practice. As the size of ships increased, the need for deepening the mouth of the river became more and more urgent. Various means were tried: in 1837 Army engineers experimented with bucket-dredging, and in 1868 a steam dredge was constructed which stirred mud to the surface where it could be carried away by the current. Dredging, however, was at best a temporary expedient, and costly besides. In 1873 Captain James B. Eads, a construction engineer with a brilliant reputation (he had designed ironclads in the Civil War, invented a successful diving bell, and built the first bridge across the Mississippi, at St. Louis), studied the situation and recommended a system of parallel jetties not unlike those Pauger had suggested. Army engineers were skeptical, but Eads finally succeeded in persuading them: Congress authorized the project rather reluctantly, requiring a partial subsidy for it out of Eads's own pocket and stipulating that he was not to be paid in full for his work until a test period of ten years should prove that the channel maintained its depth. In 1875 the work began. Eads built up a pair of parallel walls on the bottom of South Pass, using for his materials stone, piling, debris, and willow mattresses. The current was forced into the channel thus formed, deepening it to a degree that enabled even the largest ocean-going vessel to navigate it safely. At last the problem was solved: Eads's channel, a thousand feet wide and thirty-five feet deep, has been used successfully ever since July 8, 1879, the day he completed his job.

Floods constituted another problem. Levees had been constructed along the New Orleans riverfront as early as 1727, and by 1835 planters on both sides of the river, anxious to protect their crops, had extended these barriers to a point thirty miles above the city and twelve miles below. In doing so, however, they overlooked a rather obvious topographical truth: when you narrow the flow of a river you raise its flood plane, and the planters soon discovered that they were inviting the very disaster they sought to avert. Levees forced the water higher, no doubt about it; on the other hand, levees were indispensable. The problem looked insoluble, and it was made worse by the fact that the flood potential of the Mississippi, with its maze of tributaries, is far greater than that of most rivers: the melting snows of some thirty states swell it to a degree that is really menacing.

This state of affairs continued from the eighteenth century right on down into the present one. There was occasional help from the Federal Government (the floods of 1912, 1913, 1917, and 1922 caused damage amounting to many millions of dollars, and Congress passed two acts appropriating funds for flood control), but not until the spring of 1927 was the national conscience fully aroused. That year the entire Delta was submerged: the loss of life was appalling; 100,000 men, women, and children were left destitute overnight, dependent upon the Red Cross for survival; and property damage was estimated at something like $236,000,000. In order to save New Orleans, the levee had been dynamited at a point several miles below the city.

Congress now acted swiftly. An elaborate new system of levees was devised, and, more importantly, a system of floodways was installed at strategic points along the course of the river which would direct the water into areas where it could do no harm. In 1935 the Bonnet Carré Spillway, a dike-enclosed runway which shuttled floodwater into Lake Pontchartrain and thence into the Gulf of Mexico, was constructed about thirty miles above New Orleans. When it was put to use, two years later, it worked like a charm, and most New Orleanians feel it was a bargain at thirty-five million dollars.

Until 1935 there were no bridges across the Mississippi in the New Orleans area; now there are two, and their construction, what with the soft, oozy bottom of the river and the swiftness of its current, posed unusual difficulties. The Huey P. Long Bridge, which is a highway-railroad combination spanning the river about ten miles above the city limits, was many years in building and cost thirteen million dollars. It is four and a half miles long, and the height of the central pier, from the bottom of its foundation to its tip, is 499 feet, the equivalent of a thirty-six-story building: you have the illusion, when you look down from this part of the bridge, of being in an airplane. The roadway itself is 135 feet above high-water level; there is a narrow two-foot sidewalk for pedestrians, and the walk across and back is a popular one with people of athletic inclination. Jumping off this bridge is a favorite local way of committing suicide; people started doing it from almost the very day it was opened.

The Huey P. Long Bridge is on the main highway leading west and thus facilitated traffic (which has always been heavy) with the Texas cities, but for New Orleanians who simply wanted to get across the river to Algiers or Gretna it was easier to ferry across at Canal or Jackson Avenue than to drive so far upriver and return on the opposite side. A bridge was badly needed which would connect these towns with the heart of the city. The new Mississippi River Bridge, opened in April, 1958, supplies this need: a little over two miles long, it rises 170 feet in the air and has the world's largest cantilever span (1,575 feet). It is one of the most dramatically beautiful of all American bridges—as well it might be, for it cost sixty-five million dollars. The view from it is more interesting than from the older one, for it passes directly over the docks, and, as you approach New Orleans from the opposite bank, the way it suddenly sets you down from a great height into the very center of the city is most exciting. It is proving even more popular with suicides than the other; for one thing, it is more convenient.

The biggest of all these engineering projects, a seaway from the city directly to the Gulf, was begun by the United States Corps of Engineers in December, 1957, and is expected to be completed in 1963. By-passing the Mississippi's many turns, this outlet will save forty miles between the city and the open sea: part of it will be across land, canal-wise, and part of it across the open water of the Mississippi Sound in the form of a deep artificial channel. It is a gigantic undertaking, and it is expected to cost nearly a hundred million dollars.

Rivers are expensive, no doubt about it. But they are well worth it. Last year 4,333 vessels from foreign ports entered New Orleans Harbor, not to mention 2,294 inland waterway craft, and the value of foreign cargo reached an all-time high of nearly two billion dollars. Wharf facilities, in fact, have proved inadequate to the volume of trade, particularly the grain trade: on August 14, 1958, the *Times-Picayune* reported that twenty liners were awaiting service at the Public Grain Elevator, and sixty-eight barges were waiting to be unloaded. "Such has been the unusual congestion," the writer observed, "that about three million bushels of grain were directed to other ports, just since June 1." Of these other ports, Miami is the one offering the greatest competition, and there has been some concern lately among the local businessmen lest that city eventually outstrip New Orleans in Latin-American trade. The grain elevator, which was only recently expanded, is now undergoing further enlargement —one of several expedients which, it is hoped, will enable the port to maintain its prestige based on the total value of imports and exports: it still ranks first among Gulf ports, and second among national. It is the leading grain port in the United States.

Coffee and bananas are among the city's leading imports, and the wharves where these are unloaded present a colorful sight, with

NEW MISSISSIPPI RIVER BRIDGE (1958)

PHOTO BY DAN LEYRER

BUEN RETIRO (1840, JAMES GALLIER, SR., ARCH.)

gangs of Negro longshoremen singing while they perform their heavy and monotonous labors. Thousands of bags of coffee are unloaded annually at the Poydras Street wharf; the water here is unusually shallow and requires constant dredging. The Thalia Street wharf, nearby, is used by the United Fruit Company, and another banana company (Standard Fruit) uses a wharf below Canal, at Desire Street. The bananas are unloaded by means of ferris-wheel-type conveyors which are lowered into the hold of the ship, where workmen place the green bunches into the conveyor pockets; these pockets are then raised to the wharf, emptied, and returned to the ship's hold. Occasionally a tarantula or even a small boa constrictor will be concealed in one of the bunches and choose this moment to reveal himself: when this happens, there is always great excitement.

Another scene of waterfront activity is the Public Cotton Warehouse, near Napoleon Avenue, with its thirty-three acres of covered space and its cotton presses which have a capacity of a hundred bales an hour. At the moment, however, the busiest spot in the whole port is the Public Grain Elevator, at the foot of Bellecastle Street. Until this year, grain arrived at the elevator by rail at least as often as by barge, but in June and July of 1958 there was three times as much barge business as rail: to cope with this emergency, the elevator has been working on a twenty-four-hour schedule, has installed new equipment, and has revised its tariff to permit grain to be transported directly from barge to ship. Another barge-unloading berth is now under construction, the size of the sacking plant is being increased thirty-three per cent, and additional storage space is being created to accommodate more than two million bushels of grain.

There are attractive drives both up and down the river from New Orleans, and their interest is increased by an occasional plantation house surviving from the last century, when the banks of both sides were lined with such houses—spaced, of course, at considerable intervals from one another. Most of them have disappeared, and those which remain are often in a dreadful state of dilapidation; some, however, have been restored successfully and are at least safe to visit.

On the east bank, the drive down to Violet, about twelve miles below the city, is perhaps the most rewarding, not merely scenically but historically as well, for you pass the battlefield at Chalmette where Jackson repulsed the British in 1814. Beyond Chalmette the road takes you through an almost incredibly lush countryside—the rich alluvial soil of the Mississippi in this area makes for a fertility which is truly fabulous, and even weeds (of which there is an abundance) flourish with a peculiar and prodigal beauty.

There are two plantation houses which you should visit if you take this drive; they are both slightly off the main highway, since they face directly on the river, from which the road is separated by a mile or so, but the effort is worth making. They are Three Oaks and Buen Retiro, also known as the René Beauregard house. Three Oaks is just outside the city limits, in Arabi. It is the property of the American Sugar Refinery, which has restored it, and it is the very archetype of a Deep Delta plantation house—two-story, white, with galleries running all the way around it, and set back from the river at a sufficient distance so that you can get a proper view of it from the levee. The grounds are magnificent, with enormous live oaks whose moss-draped branches, to the despair of photographers, all but enclose the house from sight except from certain angles. Buen Retiro is at Chalmette, farther down the river, and stands within a stone's throw of the barricade which Jackson erected for the defense of the city. The house was not standing then, however; it was erected in the 1840's by the elder Gallier and was the home of Judge René Beauregard, the general's son. Buen Retiro corresponds a little less to the ideal pattern of a plantation house than does Three Oaks; it is marred by a crisscross railing on the upper gallery, and it has been restored rather too slickly both without and within. The building is now used as a museum for the Battle of New Orleans, and local architect Sam Wilson (who also restored Three Oaks) has succeeded only too well in divesting the air-conditioned interior of any resemblance to a home, past or present—it is all showcases, neatly printed placards, trick lighting effects, and tidy offices. But Buen Retiro looks well from a distance and is very popular with the tourists—it is much easier to photograph than Three Oaks.

At Chalmette you should also notice the long avenue of live oaks leading from the river to the ruins of the old De la Ronde plantation, Versailles, which stand like a traffic island in the exact center of the highway. Planted in 1762, these trees are among the most beautiful in the state; it would, indeed, be hard to discover finer specimens anywhere.

Across the river, on the west bank, there are two other plantation houses within easy reach: Seven Oaks and the Judah Benjamin house.

Seven Oaks is just outside Westwego, upriver, and is very nearly concealed by the cluster of oil tanks which surrounds it. It is an easy
place to miss, but to miss it would be a pity, for this house is a fine
example of Louisiana Greek Revival—large and very nearly square,
with Doric columns and a rather clumsy belvedere atop the second
story. Built about 1840 by the planter Camille Zeringue, it has been
unoccupied for many years and is badly in need of repair, though its
sturdy frame is still relatively intact. For some time now the Louisiana
Landmarks Society has been trying to persuade its owner, the Missouri Pacific Railroad, to restore Seven Oaks, and there are rumors
that work is to begin on it very soon.

The Judah Benjamin house—what is left of it—is downriver at
Belle Chasse. It is later than the other houses, and bigger: three stories,
with twenty rooms (each, naturally, with its own fireplace), lofty
ceilings, and hallways sixteen feet wide. There is an exquisite winding
staircase (from which vandals, presumably, have stripped the rail and
spindles) leading from the entrance hall all the way up to the third
floor: it is the aesthetic center and focus of the entire house, which
seems almost to have been built around it for the sole purpose of showing it off properly. There were plans to make a Civil War museum of
the Benjamin house (Judah P. Benjamin was Secretary of State for the
Confederacy before he was exiled to England, where he achieved international fame as a jurist and received a knighthood from Queen Vic-
toria), but nothing seems to have come of them. The mansion is in
a really shocking condition: the interior has been stripped of its man-
tels and moldings, while a whole balcony has collapsed outside.

What is happening to Seven Oaks and the Judah Benjamin house
is happening to many of the ante-bellum houses which are left in
Louisiana—most of them have already disappeared. It is easy to be
indignant over such a state of affairs, but these places do present a
problem. Who has use nowadays for a house with twenty or thirty
rooms? The cost of restoration, besides, is usually too great to be
borne by a single individual. Some houses, like Three Oaks, have been
restored by the big companies on whose land they happen to be located; the big companies, however, have not always proved so solici-
tous and are also responsible for the destruction of some of the finest
plantation houses in the New Orleans area. Other old houses, like the
eighteenth century Sarpy mansion on Howard Avenue (which had
the misfortune to lie in the path of the new Mississippi River Bridge),

have been leveled, in the name of progress, to make way for large-scale civic developments. The extent to which expedience should allow itself to be compromised by historical and aesthetic considerations is essentially a moral question, and businessmen are not always conspicuous for their morals.

The Lake

LAKE PONTCHARTRAIN is the largest of three lakes, all of them connected; it lies between Lake Maurepas on the west and Lake Borgne on the east. Lake Borgne is not, properly speaking, a lake at all, but a bay of the Gulf of Mexico, so that the water in Lake Pontchartrain, which is joined to it by a strait known as the Rigolets, is semisalt, which gives the lake an ambiguous identity making for variety: salt-water fish are found in it as well as fish which cannot live in salt water. The saline content, however, is not very noticeable except after storms in the Gulf, or when the water level is unusually low.

Pontchartrain has an area of six hundred square miles and is approximately forty miles long by twenty-four miles wide. It is unusually shallow for such a large body of water—sixteen feet at its deepest point—with the result that its waves are short and choppy and a strong wind will whip them into a frenzy in no time at all: small craft are always being overturned in this way, and the loss of life is greater than you might suppose.

The lake was discovered by Iberville, who named it after the French Minister of Marine, and it was a very important factor in deciding the site of New Orleans, for communication to the city at that time was mostly from the lake by way of Bayou St. John rather than from the river, which (because of the current) took much longer to navigate. Pontchartrain's shallowness posed a problem for larger vessels, but the lake route to the Gulf of Mexico and to the earliest settlements on it (Biloxi and Mobile) was much more direct. Only five miles separate the lower curve of the Mississippi from the southern shore of Lake Pontchartrain, and it was precisely at this

129

point, where the distance between river and lake was narrowest, that Bienville founded his city. Today there are two navigable water routes into the city, exclusive of the Mississippi River: the Industrial Canal, which runs through Gentilly and directly connects the lake with the river; and the more recent Intracoastal Canal, which, by-passing both Lake Pontchartrain and Lake Borgne, enters directly into the Gulf of Mexico.

Because of the drainage problem, New Orleans built up more slowly toward the lake than it did in other directions, but now the entire area has been filled in, and the lakeshore neighborhoods (Lakeview, Lake Vista, and Lake Terrace) are among the handsomest residential sections of the city. The houses in these subdivisions are mostly ranch type, long and low, with enormous picture windows and barbecue pits in the back yards—the décor is strictly one of outdoor living. Some of them are very attractive, but except for certain minor variations they all tend to look a great deal alike, and the neighborhood for this reason lacks real distinction: I should think one would have to live for months in one of these houses before one could find one's way back to it without a compass—the neighborhood is so very large, and all the streets, too, look exactly alike. The general effect is one of flatness and prosperous monotony.

For generations the southern shore of Lake Pontchartrain has provided New Orleanians with recreation in the form of boating, swimming, fishing, and crabbing (the lake crabs are particularly succulent); and nowadays, of course, you have water skiing and skin diving as well. Resort areas are scattered all along the coast: there is Bucktown, in Jefferson Parish; there is West End; there is Pontchartrain Beach; there is Milneburg; there is Lincoln Beach. The most popular of these is Pontchartrain Beach, which has an enormous midway with scores of concessions and every type of mechanical ride conceivable. There is a rather pretty public beach of white sand—it looks more like a seashore than a lakeshore—but the water is usually too warm to be really refreshing, and, particularly on weekends, is none too clean: if you are afraid to take chances you should use the big new pool which reeks reassuringly of chlorine.

Pontchartrain Beach is thronged nearly every night for four months out of the year: there are all sorts of inducements to lure the public—free vaudeville which features breathtaking acrobatic stunts high overhead; beauty contests for men and women alike ("Mr. New

Orleans" is elected here annually); and special days when the rides cost only a nickel and sometimes nothing at all, these last occasions being sponsored by the local radio and TV stations as advertisement. Considering the crowds which flock here, it is rather remarkable how bright and fresh the place always manages to look; it has nothing of the trampled, tawdry quality of a Coney Island. Sexuality, of course, is omnipresent, almost as much as in the French Quarter: there are the same frankly appraising stares, and couples make love on the beach (and in the water) in broad daylight.

Like Santa Monica, Pontchartrain Beach is the rendezvous of body-builders and weightlifters from all over the local area: on weekdays they train at places like the elaborate new International Health Studio on Camp Street, the New Orleans Health Studio on Gravier, and the American Health Studio in Metairie; and on weekends they work out on the beach—flexing their monstrous biceps, inflating their chests, and striking grotesque poses for the cameras which are sure to be clicking all around them, for they are invariably the center of an admiring group.

For those who dislike the midway atmosphere there are two other beaches, rather less crowded and quite close by: at West End, and right next to the Coast Guard station between West End and Pont-chartrain Beach. In fact, the whole shore line between West End and Pontchartrain Beach (a two-mile stretch) is suitable for swimming: the concrete seawall has been thoughtfully provided with steps from which you can wade into the water. On a hot summer evening this stretch makes a pleasant drive—the road follows the shore line within a stone's throw of the water, and there is often a breeze from the lake.

Lincoln Beach, which is for Negroes, lies several miles west of Pontchartrain Beach: integration has recently been extended to the public transportation system but not to the swimming pools or to the beaches. Lincoln Beach has expanded greatly in the last couple of years, and Negroes now use several miles of the shore line between the New Orleans Airport and the Little Woods area.

West End lies at the end of Pontchartrain Boulevard, which used to be known as Shell Road and which served as a sort of drag strip in the horse-and-buggy days. This resort has fallen into a decline since the development of Pontchartrain Beach; it is still popular with picnickers, however, and there are several seafood restaurants which do a flourishing business in the summer. There is a lighthouse and,

just opposite, the harbor of the Southern Yacht Club, which holds a
big annual regatta in April. When the weather is good, amateurs race
their sailboats here every weekend.

Just across the parish line from West End, in Jefferson, is Bucktown, a rather curious suburb with a long tradition of lawlessness behind it, like so many Jefferson Parish settlements. Bucktown is nothing more—and was never anything more—than a little cluster of bars
and restaurants and a maze of lovers' lanes, but it has an illicit atmosphere which is vaguely exciting: slot machines (which are outlawed
by the state) operate quite openly, and there is a notorious night club,
the My-O-My, which employs a staff of female impersonators some
of whom have long police records. The clientele of this establishment
is not at all what you might suppose: *outré* types are definitely in
the minority, and instead one sees the local politicians and quite re-
spectable-looking family men, sometimes with their families in tow!—
an interesting comment on the local morality. The My-O-My has
even become a sort of tourist attraction, another thing to gape at,
and it is nothing unusual to see rubberneck buses parked outside. To
come to Bucktown on a hot night and eat boiled crab and lake shrimp,
washed down with ice-cold beer, is a local custom of long standing;
Friday nights are the most popular, since this is predominantly a
Catholic town, but places like Swanson's and Fontana's are crowded
every night during the summer.

Milneburg was the northern terminus of the Pontchartrain Railroad and (while this was in operation) an important port for visitors
arriving by the lake route in the 1840's and 1850's. There was a large
hotel, the Washington, which advertised venison dinners "on arrival
of the quarter past 3 o'clock car" and whose bouillabaisse was praised
by Thackeray: "At that comfortable tavern on Pontchartrain we had
a bouillabaisse than which a better was never eaten at Marseilles, and
not the least headache in the morning, I give you my word; on the
contrary, you only wake with a sweet refreshing thirst for claret and
water." Milneburg was named after Alexander Milne, a wealthy and
eccentric Scotchman who owned a huge lakeshore estate which he
had obtained through a grant from the Spanish Government; he was
one of the first successful real-estate speculators in New Orleans, and
made a fortune when the Pontchartrain Railroad was run through a
part of his property. Milneburg was virtually his creation; he helped
lay out the streets and insisted on naming them himself—even the
inspiration for naming the town was his own. Milneburg is supposed

to have been the birthplace of Adah Menken, who thrilled audiences on both sides of the Atlantic in the middle of the nineteenth century by galloping a black horse across the stage and wearing flesh-colored tights in a performance of *Mazeppa*, an adaptation by H. M. Milner of Byron's popular poem: she is also the only woman Swinburne ever admitted having slept with.

West of Milneburg, on the mouth of Bayou St. John, is the site of the oldest fort in the New Orleans area; it was built by the Spanish in the early eighteenth century and used as a garrison during the British invasion of 1814. There is nothing to be seen now except the foundation, but the area has been referred to as Spanish Fort for many years, and it became extremely popular as a pleasure resort toward the end of the last century and the beginning of this one. Harvey Elkin, a prominent caterer, operated a large hotel there where such distinguished guests as Thackeray, Oscar Wilde, General Grant, and the Duke of Saxe-Weimar were entertained. A gambling casino and a theater which scheduled regular operatic productions were added about 1900, and for the *hoi polloi* there was a whole battery of amusement concessions—very much as you will find today at Pontchartrain Beach, only of course the rides were less ingenious and perhaps less safe.

The north shore of Pontchartrain, known as the Ozone Belt because of its pine forests, is the most healthful spot within easy reach of New Orleans: the land is relatively high and dry, and in summer the temperature is about twenty degrees cooler than in the city. During the yellow-fever epidemics there were wholesale migrations here, particularly in August and September, when the incidence of the disease was highest; and the little towns of Mandeville, Madisonville, and Covington achieved a prominence such as they had never known before and have certainly never known since.

Until two years ago, when the Pontchartrain Causeway was built connecting New Orleans and Mandeville in St. Tammany Parish, the overland route to the north shore was rather circuitous: you had to go east, cross a bridge at the narrow end of the lake, and then circle back (unless you preferred to describe the same circumlocution on the west, cutting between Lakes Maurepas and Pontchartrain). The need for a bridge directly across the lake, which would reduce this distance by half, had been realized for many years; a project was actually proposed in the twenties but was abandoned because of the expense. Now at last the bridge is a reality, and it is the longest in the

world—twenty-four miles, with two bascule spans and three humps
for marine traffic. The total length of the expressway in which it is
the main link is thirty-five miles, and the total cost was approximately
$51,000,000. It was opened, with much fanfare, on August 30, 1956.
At present there is a toll of a dollar, and the drive across and back is
more than worth the money: you have the illusion of being on a ship,
for the bridge is very low and the lake is so wide you cannot see
across it. There is almost always a breeze, and the sunsets are likely to
be spectacular.

Mandeville was founded in 1834 by the same Bernard de Marigny
who had laid out the Faubourg Marigny and named its main thoroughfare Elysian Fields; his full patronymic was Bernard Xavier
Philippe de Marigny de Mandeville, whence the name of the town.
Marigny's country estate, known as Fontainebleau, lay just east of
the town; part of it he had inherited from his father, Pierre de Marigny, but he kept adding to it until it reached the size of 3,545 acres
and extended for nine miles along the lake. Like the Faubourg Marigny, Mandeville was to be an ideal village, and Bernard supervised
the construction of its buildings and the laying out of its streets. He
instituted a ferry service from New Orleans which connected with
the recently opened Pontchartrain Railroad, imported chefs from
Paris for the new restaurants, and Mandeville became a fashionable
watering place almost overnight: gambling (for which Marigny had
a passion) was the favorite indoor pastime. "There may have been
other villages in the United States in the 1830's that equaled the
gaiety of Mandeville," writes W. Adolphe Roberts, "but there could
have been none to challenge its sophistication and European air."

Pierre de Marigny had been wise in his choice of a country estate,
and his son shrewd in expanding it: these fields were really elysian,
and there is still no pleasanter town within easy reach of New Orleans
than Mandeville, with its magnolias, its moss-draped live oaks, and
its towering pines whose spicy fragrance overhangs the whole area.
Few of the original buildings are left; most of the houses you see
have a late Victorian and Edwardian look, with fussy gingerbread
exteriors, for Mandeville continued to be popular as a resort town
for many years.

Older than Mandeville is Covington, several miles inland through
a forest of virgin pine. It was founded before the Revolution, in 1769,
and was originally called Wharton; the name was changed in 1816
as the result, it is said, of a political rally at which whisky distilled in

Covington, Kentucky, was served with more than usually exhilarating effects. Covington is the largest town in St. Tammany, and the heart of the Ozone Belt. It stands on the highest ground anywhere around here—thirty-five feet above sea level as compared to Mandeville's eleven—but it lacks the casual charm of the lakeside resort.

Madisonville, a few miles east of Mandeville and slightly inland on the Tchefuncte River, is a town which the twentieth century seems somehow to have forgotten. Its architecture is reminiscent of Mandeville, for it was built up at about the same time and attracted a good many vacationists, but Madisonville for some reason never really flourished—oddly, for its location near the mouth of the Tchefuncte would seem to favor development. It has the sleepy, antiquated look of a town that has been by-passed by the machine age; it is off the route of the big highways, and a horse and buggy would seem less incongruous on its streets than a modern automobile.

The north shore of Lake Pontchartrain is worth visiting any time, but I like it best in Indian summer. September is a sultry month in New Orleans, and the difference in temperature and humidity is most noticeable then. It is delightful to drive through these silent forests of virgin pine in the late afternoon and scent the first hint of autumn in the air: when the darkness comes it comes quickly, and you may need a sweater.

It remains to be seen how the north-shore resorts will be affected by the new bridge; as yet the only perceptible difference has been in the increase of traffic—an increase which is somewhat less than was anticipated. Yet perhaps it is merely a question of time before Mandeville begins to look like another Metairie—perhaps even dreaming, deserted Madisonville will awaken to a new life. At the moment it is hard to visualize.

The biggest excitement in St. Tammany Parish since the bridge was opened occurred a couple of months ago when an investigator from the New Orleans Police Department uncovered a nudist colony operating there. A quantity of pornographic literature was found in the possession of one of the members, and another has recently been indicted for carnal knowledge of a juvenile. There are limits, even in Elysia.

Nearby

Biloxi, on the Mississippi Gulf Coast, was the first capital of Louisiana; New Orleans was founded some twenty years later, and a close rapport existed between the two settlements from the very first: they were colonized under similar conditions and by the same national stock. For generations the Mississippi Gulf Coast has been a favorite vacation spot with New Orleanians, many of whom have built summer homes along it; and Biloxi, though it lies more than eighty miles east of New Orleans, is in a sense a suburb of the city —particularly in June, July, and August.

It is odd how this little strip of Mississippi (a state whose inhabitants, except for the Negroes, are overwhelmingly Anglo-Saxon Protestants) has managed to retain its Latin stamp, for if you go inland, even a few miles, it disappears: the family names, many of them, are still French as far up as Hattiesburg and even Meridian; these people too are of French extraction, but the religion is Baptist, the culture hillbilly, and the speech that of the Deep South backwoods (*thank* for *think*, *heel* for *hill*, *whut* for *what*, and so on). Not so on the Gulf Coast.

The drive from New Orleans to Biloxi is uninteresting for the first forty miles or so; it seems you are never going to get out of Gentilly, with its interminable string of motels, and when at last you do, you drive through flat swampland areas until you reach Bay St. Louis, the first of the Gulf Coast resorts. From then on it is sheer delight: the highway is four-lane, with a wide neutral ground, and you are within a stone's throw of the Gulf the whole way. On your left are palatial summer homes—those in the vicinity of Pass Christian are particularly impressive—and gigantic live oaks, palms, and magnolias. At Gulfport you go by Jefferson Davis's plantation house, Beauvoir, now a museum, and presently another long string of motels announces that you are nearing Biloxi. You pass a lighthouse built in 1848, about which the road divides, and find yourself in the city proper.

The first thing you notice is the beach. It is the longest man-made sand beach in the world—twenty-seven miles long and three hundred feet wide, and, perhaps because of its size, never seems really crowded, not even on the very hottest weekends. The water is shallow—you have to wade 'way out to swim, unless you use the public pier— and many visitors, particularly from the North, find it rather too warm; but it is the only genuine seashore within easy reach of New Orleans and serving a large area of the South besides, and as such is enormously popular.

Then there are the trees. Not even in New Orleans are they more beautiful, particularly the live oaks, festooned with Spanish moss and centuries old, which line the beach area—but then they are all over the town, dwarfing it and dominating it so that you are everywhere conscious of their presence. They convey a sense of peace but also of tragedy; their outlines, especially at night, are very dark and menacing. Most of all they appear wise, and, with their eternal whispering, seem to be trying to communicate to us something of their primordial intelligence. It is perhaps a fallacy to associate the idea of extreme age with wisdom, but the temptation is inevitable. One of the most spectacular of these trees is the Wallace Oak, behind the house at 848 West Beach; it is believed to be anywhere from three hundred to five hundred years old, has a circumference of twenty-two feet, and a limb which measures seventy-five feet. You should also see the avenue of live oaks which Nicholas Benachi, one-time Greek consul to New Orleans who had a summer home in Biloxi, planted here over a hundred years ago. Henry Miller has paid homage to these trees in his controversial travel book *The Air-Conditioned Nightmare:* Biloxi, he says, was the only town in America that gave him "a genuine and pleasant surprise."

Biloxi is the biggest shrimp and oyster port in the world. The local fisheries, of which there are more than twenty, operate about a thousand boats and employ twelve thousand workers: one out of every five inhabitants earns his livelihood in this way. Every year there is a shrimp festival climaxed by a religious ceremony at which a Roman Catholic priest blesses the shrimp fleet, first *en masse* and then boat by boat, intoning a ritual which is many centuries old. The boats are always gaily decorated with flags and paper streamers for this event and make a fine showing as they pass before the priest, who sprinkles them with holy water, and prizes are awarded to those having the best decorations.

Tourism is another big business here. Biloxi is not only near New Orleans, but it is also on the main highway between that city and Mobile, Pensacola, and all the Florida cities; the volume of traffic passing through it, particularly in the summer months, is prodigious —it is a favorite stopping-over place, which explains the many tourist courts. (There are also at least three first-rate hotels right on the beach: the Buena Vista, biggest and most luxurious; the White House; and the Trade Winds.) But many people rent cottages for the whole summer: the deep-sea fishing season opens in April and is attracting more sportsmen every year; by the time July comes around the houses are all rented, you need advance reservations at the hotels, and the motels flash their neon "No Vacancy" signs.

Keesler Field, the electronics center of the United States Air Force, is located in Biloxi. About twenty thousand men are stationed here at the moment, but during World War II it accommodated nearly seventy thousand: the native population of Biloxi at that time numbered only about twenty-five thousand, an inequality making for occasional friction between civilians and soldiers; these tensions are disappearing fast, but have not altogether vanished from the local scene.

Biloxians are a gentle, soft-spoken, happy-looking people. Nature has been kind to them, favoring them with a mild climate and a location which is as beautiful as it is productive of profit. They lack the animation of New Orleanians (they are an easygoing lot, even in their pleasures), but they are less irritable and have a delightfully irrepressible sense of humor. There are some strikingly handsome physical types among them, as if they had borrowed a bit of the beauty of their surroundings. Only about sixteen per cent of the town's population is Negro, which is unusual in a state having more Negro inhabitants than white. Commercial fishing for some reason has never seemed to attract Negroes; as you go inland their number increases steadily.

Another interesting excursion out of New Orleans is to the bayou country west of the Mississippi. Crossing the new Mississippi River

Bridge to Algiers, you turn south at Harvey and drive for half an hour or so through a lonely, heavily wooded area (to the accompaniment of a deafening chorus of frogs and crickets) emerging finally at Lafitte, a tiny village on Bayou Barataria. Lafitte is an extraordinarily picturesque town: being both small and out of the way, it has managed, in spite of its proximity to New Orleans, to preserve its identity as a fishing village wonderfully well. The town lies to the right of the road, and is strung along the shore of the bayou; the ramshackle little houses, with their miniature front yards not more than twenty or thirty feet deep, face directly on the water, or rather on the little mud path (the main street of the village!) which skirts the water. Lafitte is perhaps the only town in the United States with a main street two feet wide; in places it is narrower than that, and you must tread carefully if you wish to avoid falling into the bayou. Live oaks line this unique little thoroughfare, their moss-draped limbs extending out over the water.

Nearly every house has a pirogue "parked" before it in the bayou. Pirogues are canoes hollowed out of a single cypress log, about thirteen feet long and twenty-two inches wide, and are the popular means of transportation in an area where the houses are frequently inaccessible to roads and even to footpaths. They are hard to handle, but the natives have acquired phenomenal skill in paddling, and can skim over the water in them at a speed that is really remarkable. A pirogue race is held at Lafitte every spring: thousands of people from nearby towns and New Orleans turn out to watch it, lining both banks of the bayou for the four-mile stretch which constitutes the course. It is an exciting contest, and is nearly always won by one of the local folk; several years ago a Northerner entered it and finished last, to the delight of the natives. Later on, in the summer, there is a shrimp-blessing ceremony similar to the one in Biloxi.

In the nineteenth century Lafitte was the site of a pirate settlement, and many of the inhabitants are descended from the buccaneers who sailed under Jean Lafitte and infested the maze of bayous opening into Barataria Bay. These pirates were a motley assortment, the outcasts and the scum of many nations; there were even a few Lascars and Chinese among them, and the high cheekbones and yellow skin indicative of Asiatic origin are by no means uncommon among the villagers today. Toward the end of the century, the population of Lafitte was augmented and rendered even more complex by a number of Filipino and Mexican immigrants who settled here and practiced the same occupation with which they had had experience at home. (There are immigrant colonies of this type all over the Gulf area: Biloxi has a large number of Yugoslav shrimpers, and Greek sponge fishermen are scattered all along the lower west coast of Florida, particularly in the Tarpon Springs area.) Manila Village, a few miles from Lafitte, is inhabited almost exclusively by Filipinos, who live in houses built on stilts above the water and whose rather specialized occupation is the sun-drying of shrimp on large platforms.

Grand Isle, which lies about a hundred miles southwest of New Orleans, was another pirate settlement. The trip (through Raceland, Golden Meadow, and Leeville) is an interesting one: after Golden Meadow you go through bayou country similar to that around Lafitte; the streams are full of water hyacinths—a nuisance to shrimp boats, but a beautiful sight in the spring, with their lavender blossoms. Until comparatively recent years Grand Isle was inaccessible by road; you had to make at least a part of the trip by boat, and there was only one good hotel on the island. Now there are several, and for the first time in its history Grand Isle is beginning to attract tourist trade, with the result that prices have soared during the summer season. The fishing is remarkably good, especially deep-sea fishing, and there is a big annual Tarpon Rodeo.

Grand Isle is seven miles long and a mile and a half wide; it has a rather attractive natural sand beach, but offshore oil drilling (a big industry now on the Louisiana coast) makes it unsuitable for swimming. There are groves of live oaks whose shapes have been grotesquely distorted by strong winds, so that they all lean in the direction of the mainland. (Hurricanes are a problem on Grand Isle; there was a particularly severe one in 1956 from which the island has not yet quite recovered.) The landward side is rather heavily wooded with the usual semitropical plants: palm, palmetto, Spanish dagger, yaupon, elderberry, chinaberry, and—perhaps most plentiful of all—oleander. The streets are called lanes, and the yards of the little frame cottages are fragrant with four-o'-clock and night-blooming jasmine.

Fishing is the biggest local industry, as it is the chief local sport, but there is also considerable muskrat trapping here as elsewhere in the Barataria region. Louisiana produces something like six million muskrat pelts a year, which is three times the number produced by the rest of the United States *and* Canada: mink, fox, otter, and raccoon are also quite common. During the brief duck and geese season (November 26th to Christmas Day) Grand Isle is a hunter's paradise.

Like the inhabitants of Lafitte, many Grand Islanders are descended from pirates—there is a Chinghizola family and a Chinghizola Lane on the island today ("Cut Nose" Chinghizola was one of Lafitte's fiercest lieutenants). A long tradition of lawlessness survives on Grand Isle, and the accident of its location in corrupt Jefferson Parish increases the strength of this tradition: gambling of all types flourishes quite openly, and the local taverns are the scene of frequent brawls. The natives here have always been suspicious of outsiders, an attitude which has slowed down tourism considerably; they are especially resentful of New Orleanians. Why this should be so is not easy to explain; it has nothing to do with economics, obviously, and may possibly be accounted for in terms of inbreeding and geographical isolation. Juvenile delinquency is a problem on Grand Isle as it is everywhere else, only here (as in the Irish Channel) the problem is aggravated by a tradition of violence: thuggery, however, is not confined to the juvenile bracket, and after dark the bars on this island are places to be avoided.

FOUR

Special Aspects

The Mardi Gras

IT is the biggest day of the year: Christmas is a holiday which New Orleans shares with other cities, but Mardi Gras is her very own. And New Orleans, at least to a Northerner, does not seem a proper setting for Christmas—snow and ice are missing, and a reindeer would be as ill at ease in the Deep Delta as a unicorn. But Mardi Gras comes in the spring, and the excitement of the day is inseparable from the excitement of the season. It had a religious meaning once, and still does to faithful Catholics in the city (being the last day before the Lenten season), but the religious meaning now is secondary to the social one: it is a day when people forget their debts, hide their everyday faces behind masks, and buy drinks for perfect strangers—though there are no strangers on Mardi Gras, for the pleasure principle makes everyone blood brother for a day.

This is the reason that Mardi Gras is the most typical of all the city's institutions. It would be inconceivable anywhere else in America: one remembers the grim fate of the maskers in Hawthorne's "The Maypole of Merry Mount," and modern Massachusetts seems scarcely more conducive to the spirit of public revelry. More than the inhabitants of most cities, New Orleanians live by the pleasure principle: the right to enjoy oneself by means of the senses is commonly conceded to be inalienable, and the greatest sin that one can possibly commit is to be unhappy. Mardi Gras in New Orleans is not a holiday; it is every day—or rather, it is one day which distills the essence of all the other days, recapitulating and symbolizing a whole way of life and a very definite attitude toward it.

It is a pagan celebration, and has its ultimate origin in paganism —in the Lupercalian rites which, in imperial Rome, degenerated into mass orgies: the first maskers were female impersonators who, following the example of the emasculated priests of Attis who wore phallic charms about their necks and practiced prostitution as a ritual, indulged quite publicly in frenzied orgies. The Lupercalia lasted three days, during which time the imperial laws were suspended and all forms of license were tolerated. With the incorporation of pagan cults into Christianity, this festival (as Sir James Frazer has shown in *The Golden Bough*) passed over into the *Carnelevamen* of the Roman Catholic Church, a period ending on Ash Wednesday.

Highly watered versions of the Roman festival survive today in the Mediterranean countries, particularly on the French and Italian rivieras, and of course the Venetian Carnival has been for many centuries an important feature of the life in that city (it is extraordinary how readily comparisons between Venice and New Orleans suggest themselves). The truth is that the idea of Carnival appeals to certain very basic urges underlying the human character. The desire to dress up occasionally in unfamiliar costume, in the garments of another period or even of the opposite sex, is latent in almost everyone, as is also the mimetic urge, to which it is closely related. Children are forever indulging these urges, which become weaker as one grows up into the matter-of-fact, endlessly complicated world of one's elders; they never disappear entirely, however. Carnivals provide an outlet for them, and a legitimate pretext: a grown man can't very well rig himself up in outlandish clothes, even in the privacy of his own home; it would be too ridiculous, and yet if everyone else agrees to do so it will strike him as an excellent idea.

Likewise with masks. The temptation to don these is so universal that there is no culture in which they have not played a part, sometimes a very important part—whether in religion, drama, art, or folk celebration of any type. This temptation is not merely the desire to be anonymous; it may also involve a wish to escape from the particular to the abstract (one recalls the tragic and comic masks worn by Greek actors), from the individual to the type, or from the human to the non-human. A mask can make anyone terrifying, as the armor-smiths of the Middle Ages well knew, or it can make a laughing stock of the most dignified of persons; and few traits are more characteristic of men than that they shall sometimes wish to appear as other than they are, whether out of expedience, or because they have something to hide, or because they are bored with their ordinary faces, or sometimes simply in a spirit of fun. The psychologists tell us that the fear of being laughed at is one of the strongest of all possible fears; but there is also, as with all strong emotions, a certain perverse attraction in the opposite direction—in the direction, that is, of occasionally being *laughed at*, and masks have the power to provide us with this strange satisfaction at the same time that they render us anonymous: we save our faces by concealing them, with the thought that people are not laughing at us but at our masks. There are, of course, less recondite explanations than these for the popularity of masks—such as the ease with which they facilitate illicit amours, and here one is again reminded of the Venetians, for whom this motive was perhaps predominant.

In any event, the pagan tradition of Carnival, introduced here by the French in the eighteenth century, took unusually firm root in the fertile soil of Louisiana and flourished triumphantly in its semi-tropical climate; it could not possibly have found more ideal conditions for its survival. On Mardi Gras the local police, like the Roman, have adopted a hands-off policy—though here it is done out of necessity, as there aren't enough of them to go around—and sexuality in all its forms is still the order of the day: there are frequent violations of public decency, but they are usually in the interest of humor, besides which everybody is too busy having a good time to be really indignant. The use of confetti at the parades is relatively recent; all through the last century people scattered flour instead—another survival straight from pagan Rome, where wheat was an important fertility symbol. The sacrifice of a bull was another feature of the Lupercalia, and the custom of leading a steer, a *bœuf gras*, through the street as part of the Rex parade survived well into the twentieth century: the animal was later slaughtered, and his haunches provided the royal court with excellent roasts.

Considering that there is so little official interference, it is surprising how few crimes occur on Mardi Gras—a few cases of pickpocketing and an occasional holdup; it is hardly ever anything more serious. It was not always so: there was so much violence during the Spanish administration that public masking was forbidden by the authorities. But Mardi Gras now has become so universal an institution in the city that even hoodlums are not immune to the contagion of harmless gaiety which rages through it on that occasion; after all, one can steal any day of the year, and even thieves must have their moments of relaxation: on another day the rubber masks will be donned for a more sinister purpose. It is true that you see occasional fights, particularly late in the evening of the big day, when people begin to feel their liquor, and occasionally the teen-age gangs will roam the streets looking for trouble; there is some pushing and pulling, inevitable among people packed so closely together on the streets, but on the whole the crowd is a good-natured one.

The excitement in the air on Mardi Gras day is an almost tangible thing—it is a substance you inhale from the confetti-strewn atmosphere, that you drink from a bottle of beer or Coca-Cola, that you absorb from your morning doughnuts and the ham and potato salad which it is traditional for you to eat at lunch. There is no escaping it, whether you are wearing a costume or not. Everybody participates—rich and poor, black and white, children and adults, Catholics and Protestants, priests and libertines, convent girls and B-girls. It is a day when all barriers (of age, of race, of religion, of wealth, of morals, of profession) are lowered, when anyone consorts with everyone, and when a smile is the only thing that is absolutely *de rigueur*.

Although the custom came to New Orleans in the eighteenth century, it did not really catch on until the last one: balls and public masking had taken place more or less regularly since 1766, but the first formal parade was held in 1838. On Ash Wednesday of that year the *Daily Picayune* commented: "In the procession were several carriages superbly ornamented—bands of music, horses richly caparisoned, personations of knights, cavaliers, heroes, demigods, chanticleers, punchinellos, etc., all mounted. Many of them were dressed in female attire, and acted the lady with no small degree of grace."

Mardi Gras nearly died out in the 1850's. Rowdyism had become so serious a problem that many citizens were afraid to leave their homes, and masked toughs from the Irish Channel roamed the Negro neighborhoods (the Irish immigrants detested the Negroes because they would work for lower wages), beating up and sometimes killing their inhabitants. Then in 1854, while a Carnival ball was in progress at the Théâtre d'Orléans, a whole balcony collapsed, and many revelers lost their lives. This happened shortly before Mardi Gras day, and that year the *Bee* reported that "only boys with bags of flour paraded the streets, and painted Jezebels exhibited themselves in public carriages." The newspapers predicted the end of Carnival, but in 1857, quite unexpectedly, citizens were treated to the sight of the most lavish parade yet—that of the Mistick Krewe of Comus, which is the oldest of all the many Carnival organizations in the city today. The procession took place on the evening of Mardi Gras day, and was followed by a spectacular masquerade ball at the Gaiety Theater. The pattern thus established, of a parade followed by a ball, soon became firmly fixed, and the organizations multiplied rapidly; now there are dozens of them.

The occupation of New Orleans by Union forces during the Civil War dampened the hilarity of the occasion somewhat: in 1867 a Federal official, wearing a scarlet clown's suit, was found murdered, and after that all parades except that of Comus were forbidden, and masking after dark was also banned by the city authorities. (It is still traditional for street revelers to unmask in the evening, though it is now a custom and not a law—a custom, too, which many violate.) In 1873, during the unpopular Reconstruction administration of Henry Clay Warmoth, the subject of the Comus parade was "The Missing Links to Darwin's 'Origin of Species,' " and the procession had not gone many blocks before the public realized that it was an elaborate satire on the Federal administration: each "missing link" was an important Union official—a hyena wore a mask resembling General Butler, a tobacco grub was made up to look like President Grant, and so on. This parade ended in chaos and had to be disbanded before it reached its final destination. Two years later, in 1875, Mardi Gras was banned by General Philip H. Sheridan, who feared the occasion might result in a battle such as had taken place in September of the previous year between the White League and the metropolitan police (some of the Carnival krewes were composed largely of White Leaguers). It was resumed in 1876, however, and has been interrupted since then only twice: in 1918 and 1919 because of the First World War, and in 1942–1945 because of the Second.

The season proper opens on Twelfth Night, though one organization (the Harlequins) jumps the gun by holding a ball on New Year's Eve. Balls continue all through January, spaced a day or two apart to give the debutantes a chance to catch their breath; it is a kind of warm-up for the following month, when there is at least one ball every night. Mardi Gras is a movable date, dependent upon Easter, but it normally comes in the third or fourth week of February or the first week of March. The last ball, that of Comus, is held on the evening of Mardi Gras day; it is the most brilliant and the most exclusive of them all. Mardi Gras always falls on a Tuesday (*Mardi Gras* is French for "Fat Tuesday"), and in New Orleans the term is also sometimes used to apply to a masker: in this sense it has become part of the local vocabulary—thus, Mrs. X might say to Mrs. Y, "Where does Mrs. Z get such odd-looking clothes? I saw her yesterday, looking like a Mardi Gras."

The spirit of Mardi Gras is essentially democratic; it was a people's holiday in Rome, and when it was introduced to New Orleans it retained its popular character for a time. Mardi Gras day has always been one of public celebration here, but with the advent of the big organizations in the latter half of the nineteenth century (Momus, Proteus, Rex, and Comus), the Carnival season as a whole was one which only a select few could enjoy: the balls were limited to members of these organizations and their guests. This is the reason why these societies have increased so very rapidly—now there are so many that everyone can belong to one or another of them, and Mardi Gras has returned to the people. Attendance is still by invitation, but there is no one nowadays who cannot manage to secure one somewhere; they are all over the place. Among what may be termed the Old Guard of New Orleans, however (and by this is meant the members of the Boston and Orleans clubs), the old distinctions still persist, and for a debutante to be recognized at one of the newer balls would be as effective a way to commit social suicide as to take a Negro lover: masks, of course, simplify matters somewhat.

Rex is the biggest of all the organizations, and the King and Queen of Rex are the official monarchs of Mardi Gras; they are usually a prominent businessman and a debutante, and their identities are not revealed until Mardi Gras morning, when it comes out in the papers. Rex was founded in 1872, the year in which Grand Duke Alexis Romanoff Alexandrovitch visited the city to participate in the merry-making, and a favorite song of the duke's, "If Ever I Cease to Love" (from H. B. Farnie's *Blue Beard*, which the duke had heard Lydia Thompson sing at the Academy of Music), has become the official Carnival anthem. Each organization has its own King and Queen, however, and its own court: hierarchy within hierarchy.

The parades are dazzling, particularly the night parades. Some, of course, are more spectacular than others, but the floats and costumes generally are of a quality so superior to those of public processions in other cities as to make comparisons pointless and even absurd:

enormous sums, paid out of the members' dues, go into their preparation, and work on them begins almost a year in advance. Formerly the *papier-mâché* patterns on the floats, the costumes, the jewels, and even the ball invitations were made in France; now only the royal jewels come from Paris.

The floats are built on wheeled carts which until fairly recently were drawn by horses; diminutive tractors are used now. They must not be so long and so wide that they cannot manipulate street corners, nor so tall that they will interfere with telephone wires, but these are the only limitations which the designer must observe. Working from his models, carpenters erect wooden frames on top of the carts and fit them onto the *papier-mâché* forms which the subject calls for—mountains, castles, animals, and so on. Iron rods are placed here and there on the floats as supports for the maskers who stand on them, tossing trinkets to the crowd; the superstructure has a way of swaying dangerously when the cart is in motion, so that the maskers sometimes have to hold on for dear life: nearly every year somebody gets drunk and falls off.

For its parade, an organization will naturally choose a subject with many pictorial possibilities which enable the designer to make fullest use of his imagination. Standard works of literature make favorite subjects: Dante's *Inferno*, with terrifying *papier-mâché* flames and the damned souls writhing in agony; Homer's *Iliad* and *Odyssey*, complete with sirens and a one-eyed giant; Theseus threading his way through marvelous labyrinths to slay the Minotaur; the *Morte d'Arthur*, with its dragons and Launcelot holding high the Golden Grail; and *Alice in Wonderland*, with the magic mirror, the Queen of Hearts, the March Hare, and Alice herself, wearing a wig of long blonde hair and a mask that gives her a curiously sexless look. Mythology and history are also popular sources: "The Gods of Ancient Greece," "The Voyages of Marco Polo," "Columbus Discovering America," "Rome Under the Caesars," "The Italian Renaissance," and so on. I still remember with a thrill of horror a float which I saw as a child depicting the execution of Mary, Queen of Scots (I think the subject of the parade was "The History of England"): the axe was gigantic, ten times as awful as the real weapon could possibly have been, and blood, of course, was everywhere—the whole float was daubed with it.

Night parades are the most exciting. Everyone eats an early dinner, for they start promptly at seven from the "dens" on Calliope Street where the floats have been prepared, proceed downtown to the business district by a traditional route, pass on both sides of Canal Street, go down Royal Street into the French Quarter as far as Orleans, where they turn left to the Municipal Auditorium, and here they disband for the big ball which follows. Negroes in red robes march alongside the floats for the entire distance, occasionally performing cakewalk steps and carrying gasoline torches, flambeaux, and sparklers, while various city bands provide the music: there is no rest for band musicians during the Carnival season.

The best place to see a parade is from a balcony—a French Quarter balcony, preferably, if you know someone who has one, for these hang directly over the narrow streets and increase your chances of catching one of the glass-bead necklaces for which grown men and women scramble as eagerly as if they were genuine jewels from Tiffany: you have never seen anything like it. The worst thing you can say about a parade is that it ran out of trinkets (which sometimes happens) or that the maskers were stingy with them: to come home from a parade empty-handed is a misfortune to be compensated for only by the hope that next time things will be different. People keep these souvenirs the year round, sometimes hanging them, together with their St. Christopher medals, on the mirrors of their cars.

Children, of course, are ecstatic, what with all the balloons, the confetti, the peanuts, the cold drinks, the popcorn, the hot dogs, the cotton candy, and the apples-on-a-stick. Those whom no amount of threatening or cajoling could persuade to eat their early dinners suddenly develop enormous appetites, which they forget as soon as the shriek of motorcycle sirens, the blare of marching music, and the reddish glow of flambeau torches announce that the parade is at last approaching. In the street, where people line up six and eight rows deep, everyone pushes his child to the front: they cannot get close enough to the flambeaux bearers, and nobody objects—it is a privilege of the very young and the very small. Their eyes are enormous. No one enters more readily into the spirit of Mardi Gras than very young children, to whom it must appear one of the very few occasions when grownups act as if they had sense.

The oldest of the big Carnival organizations which hold parades today are Momus, Proteus, Rex, and Comus. Momus parades on the Thursday before the big day, Proteus the following Monday evening, Rex at noon Tuesday, and Comus Tuesday night. Hermes and Babylon, which are more recent, also hold big night parades, and on Mardi

Gras day there is a whole galaxy of processions all over town: the biggest of these is the one held by a Negro organization known as the Zulus. The Negroes have always loved Mardi Gras, and the parade of the grass-skirted Zulu King, which precedes that of Rex on Mardi Gras day, is probably the liveliest in town; his ball certainly is. In 1949 Louis Armstrong fulfilled a lifelong ambition by serving as King of the Zulus.

The best places to see the street masking on Mardi Gras are Canal Street, where the crowds are thickest, and Bourbon Street, where they are scarcely less so and where (perhaps because the French Quarter is a kind of artists' center) the costumes are particularly ingenious; sometimes, too, they are very beautiful and very expensive. But Bourbon Street on Mardi Gras is no place for the squeamish. The masking here takes on an extremely uninhibited, even a downright bawdy quality—Adam and Eve may stroll by at any moment, wearing nothing but a pair of rather insecurely fastened fig leaves. Of course, the weather may have something to say about that, even if the police don't: February in New Orleans can be cruelly chilly, and most dedicated maskers have two sets of costumes from which they may choose. The costumes in the Negro neighborhoods are also likely to be spectacular; many Negroes will save for months in order to do themselves justice on Mardi Gras. They are especially fond of exotic, brilliantly colored outfits—North Rampart Street is full of plumed Oriental princes, Queens of Sheba, and Red Indian chieftains.

Pagan in its origins, perverse (or rather complex) in its psychology, unrestrained in its manifestations—Mardi Gras is a phenomenon in twentieth century Christian America. There is no other city in America where it could succeed on such a scale; even the celebrations in Mobile and Biloxi are rather halfhearted affairs. And the scale on which it does succeed is overwhelming: Mardi Gras is a big business here, a business from which the whole city profits in one way or another; hotels, restaurants, and shops profit most directly, of course. It is not, actually, the best time to visit the city, at least from the standpoint of weather: April is a more reliable month, and in February it is certainly easier to lean back and listen to Columbia's recording of Milhaud's *Carnival in New Orleans*, based on Creole tunes, which marvelously reproduces the excitement of the event. The crowds are a bit of a nuisance, too, except on Mardi Gras day, when you accept them as part of the fun; at other times they make for a good many inconveniences. Yet if you visit New Orleans at

Mardi Gras you will be seeing its most characteristic aspect: in the language of algebra, you will be seeing the spirit of the city raised to its highest power, for Mardi Gras is an accurate symbol of both the place and the people—a place where almost anything can happen and a people who value nothing quite so much as a good time.

The Food

At that comfortable tavern on Pontchartrain we had a bouillabaisse than which a better was never eaten even at Marseilles: and not the least headache in the morning, I give you my word; on the contrary, you only wake with a sweet refreshing thirst for claret and water.

—WILLIAM MAKEPEACE THACKERAY, *Roundabout Papers*

CONSIDERING that Thackeray was an authority on bouillabaisse, and had even written a poem on the subject, this is high praise. A notorious gourmand (overeating eventually caused his death), Thackeray was delighted generally with the food in New Orleans: of all the cities in the world, he said, this was the one "where you could eat the most and suffer the least."

In an age of cafeterias and drive-in hamburger emporiums, New Orleans is still one of the few cities in America where the art of cooking has not degenerated and where it is assumed that one has a palate as well as a stomach. Not that cafeterias and hamburger stands do not exist—the town is full of them, and getting fuller all the time, but you will find even in these places that the quality of the food is exceptional, far higher than that of comparable establishments in other parts of the country: the homely hamburger, with just the right *soupçon* of seasoning, becomes a real delicacy in the hands of a New Orleans short-order cook, and even crowded drugstores in the business district serve food which compares favorably with that in the bona fide restaurants of certain other American cities. And if you should eat at one of the really first-class restaurants, like Antoine's or Galatoire's—or, better still, if you should happen to be invited to dinner in a Creole home—you will be served such food as cannot be duplicated anywhere else in the world, not even in Paris.

It is easy to overstate the case. New York has a far greater variety of excellent restaurants—the greatest variety, perhaps, of any city in the world, and even for French food it will be very hard to surpass Le Pavillon anywhere; Chicago and Kansas City are not to be outdone in the matter of steaks, nor is San Francisco in the particular kind of seafood that abounds on the West Coast. But it is quite possible in all of these cities to eat very poor food for which one can pay high prices; it is not impossible in New Orleans, but it is not very likely to happen—the chances are overwhelmingly against it, and this is because there is here, as there is in Paris, a tradition of eating well, and because there exists, as a consequence, a discriminating public palate. It is not a city in which a gourmet of catholic tastes would wish to live indefinitely—there is not a single really good Italian restaurant in New Orleans—but it is the only city in the United States where shrimp, crabs, crawfish, redfish, pompano, and flounder are cooked in such a variety of good ways. Nowhere in Europe or America can you get a bowl of Creole gumbo such as Antoine's serves, nor such succulent oysters Rockefeller, nor such pompano *en papillote*—not at the Tour d'Argent, nor at the Lapérouse, nor at Le Pavillon. Creole cooking is highly specialized, which is one reason why it is inimitable, and another one is that some of the basic ingredients (like the Gulf pompano and the crawfish) and a few of the seasonings (like the *filé* powder used in gumbos) are difficult if not impossible to obtain elsewhere: *filé* powder is hard to get now even in New Orleans.

Although the dishes have French names, it is not French cooking (whatever *that* is, including, as it does, cuisines so diverse as the Basque, the Norman, and the Provençal). The bouillabaisse that so delighted Thackeray probably bore little resemblance to the specialty of Marseilles, and I have known Frenchmen who ordered chicken *à la bonne femme* to raise their brows at what was finally set before them in the local restaurants (their consternation, I should add, was almost invariably short-lived). It is not even eighteenth century French cooking, like the *habitant* cuisine on the Gaspé—the cooking in France has changed considerably since the eighteenth century, while in Canada it has (like the language) survived in isolation. Nor is it Spanish either: where are the olive oil, the saffron, and the pimientos? It was originally French, eighteenth century French, that is, adapted to Colonial surroundings which required the substitution of wild duck for tame geese, and oysters for mussels. Except for the emphasis on rice, which could be cultivated here as easily as in Valencia, the Spanish domination did not affect the local cooking any more than it affected the local language: its greatest influence was on the architecture. More important were the innovations introduced by African slaves and by the Indians, with their strange stews and spices (*filé* powder was a product of the Choctaws, who used to sell it in the French Market). It would be hard to conceive of anything more hybrid, and further removed from contemporary European or American dishes, than such typical Creole concoctions as gumbo, or jambalaya, or courtbouillon.

There is no standard recipe for Creole gumbo—or for any of the famous New Orleans dishes, for that matter. There are certain basic ingredients, but the proportions in which they are combined is a matter of individual discretion: the dish is as good as the cook is skillful, and a good Creole cook never measures anything; he doesn't need to, relying upon taste as his sole criterion. Even the basic materials may vary: gumbo, which is a very thick soup poured over fluffy steamed rice, may be made with shrimp, with oysters, with crabs, or with any combination of these (and if there is a bit of ham lying around the kitchen it is added also), while chicken gumbo requires no seafood at all. The term *gumbo* is a generic one, and there are only a few specific requirements: it should be prepared in a heavy pot, preferably one of iron; it should include, in addition to the seafood or chicken and the basic oil-and-flour *roux*, a bit of green pepper, onion, parsley, tomato, and a bay leaf or two; it should be thickened to the right consistency with either *filé* powder or okra slices; and it must be served with rice.

Rice is of course a staple in Louisiana, and it forms the basis of many dishes in New Orleans. Served with red beans (which have been simmered for hours with a bit of ham or salt pork, a couple of bay leaves, and other seasonings), it makes an inexpensive and substantial workingman's dish, perhaps the most popular in the city, and is traditionally served with garlic bread and beer. You should try this at Kolb's, on St. Charles Street near Canal. Jambalaya, another rice dish, is perhaps of Spanish origin: its resemblance to *paella* is probably too close to be merely accidental. Like gumbo, its contents vary, depending upon the contents of the kitchen; usually it is made of shrimp, oysters, pork sausage, or ham, which is placed in an iron pot together with rice, tomatoes, onion, garlic, parsley, thyme, bay leaves, salt and pepper and cooked over a slow fire until the liquid is absorbed and the rice is soft and dry. Still another popular rice dish is shrimp *à la Creole*, a thick shrimp-and-tomato stew poured over dry steamed rice and served with garlic bread and a bottle of chilled sauterne or Chablis: it makes an ideal luncheon, and Galatoire's, on Bourbon Street, serves the best in town.

Crabs and shrimp are cooked in a variety of ways, the simplest of which is by boiling them in a pot of water seasoned with dried herbs (packages of which can be bought in all the local groceries); they are then refrigerated and served cold in the shell. This is a favorite way of eating them in the summer, served with beer and soda crackers: the natives have developed extraordinary skill in shelling them, but it is a pretty messy business for anyone, and you had better tuck a napkin under your chin when you go about it. Crawfish are also served this way during their brief springtime season. New Orleanians like their oysters on the half-shell, and there are oyster bars all over town; those in the lobby of Gluck's Restaurant on Royal Street and at Felix's on Iberville are among the best in the business area. But they are also popular fried, and half a dozen of them in this form served on half a loaf of lightly buttered French bread, with a dash of ketchup and a slice of pickle and lemon, makes an adequate lunch for an office worker. Oysters Rockefeller were invented by Jules Alciatore of Antoine's Restaurant (he was Antoine Alciatore's son) and named in honor of John D. Rockefeller on the occasion of that gentleman's visit to his restaurant; they are oysters baked on the half-shell in a covering made of buttered bread crumbs and finely ground spinach, lettuce, parsley, green onions, chervil, and tarragon leaves: this exotic mixture is pressed through a sieve and poured over the oysters, which are then placed in pie pans lined with rock salt (to preserve the heat) and put into the oven.

There is an enormous variety of fish dishes, too, of which none is more interesting than pompano *en papillote*. Pompano, which is peculiar to the Gulf of Mexico, is one of the most delicately flavored of all fish (Mark Twain said it was "as delicious as the less criminal forms of sin"), and the paper bag in which it is baked allows it to retain the full integrity of its flavor: the fish is covered with a sauce made of cream, shrimp, crab flakes, and spiced egg yolks and baked for ten minutes in a hot oven; when it emerges, the bag is puffed up like a balloon. (The dish was invented, also by Jules Alciatore, in honor of the balloonist Alberto Santos-Dumont when he came to New

Orleans early in the present century.) Antoine's is still the best place to eat pompano *en papillote*, but Arnaud's is a very close second.

Trout is also very popular. Arnaud's serves a marvelous trout *meunière*, with a butter sauce, and at Antoine's the trout *amandine* (baked with a butter-and-almond covering) is a perennial favorite. But in the matter of trout the honors go to Galatoire's—a restaurant, by the way, where it is quite impossible not to eat well provided one knows what to order. Galatoire's makes—and has made for generations—a trout *Marguéry* which is truly memorable: I have had it there dozens of times and have never known it to fall short of perfection. Trout *Marguéry* consists of rolled filets baked in half a glass of water for ten minutes in a hot oven; nothing sounds simpler than that, but the secret lies in what is done to it after it is taken out of the oven: it is covered with a sauce resembling a Hollandaise to which have been added shrimp, mushrooms, truffles, lemon, and a little of the water in which the fish has been baked; and it is in the judicious blending of these ingredients that the cook shows his skill and that the diner rejoices as the dish is placed before him together with a *salade verte*, a crisp hot loaf of French bread, and a bottle of chilled Chablis.

Redfish is the basis for one of the most tasty of all Creole dishes—courtbouillon. Like gumbo and jambalaya, this is cooked in an iron pot: chopped onion is first browned in a flour-and-oil *roux*, and a mixture of chopped green pepper and celery, tomatoes, parsley, thyme, allspice, bay leaves, garlic, salt, pepper, lemon, and flour is then added to the pot and allowed to simmer for half an hour, after which the fish slices are dropped in. Some fifteen minutes later, a glass of claret is added and the courtbouillon is ready; it is sometimes served, like bouillabaisse, on toast. Courtbouillon can also be made with red snapper, but the flavor of this fish is so delicate that it is apt to disappear when cooked in this manner: it is often, like salmon, boiled or poached and served cold with mayonnaise and capers; sometimes, too, it is stuffed with an oyster or shrimp-and-oyster dressing, like flounder, and baked. A good place to eat red snapper is Masson's Beach House on Pontchartrain Boulevard near the West End lakefront.

Meats are secondary to seafood in Creole cookery. It almost never occurs to me to order a steak in a restaurant such as Antoine's or Galatoire's—not because it will not be first-rate (Galatoire's are particularly good, and the Béarnaise sauce is a triumph), but because good steak is obtainable elsewhere, both in New Orleans (at the Sir-loin Room on South Claiborne, for example) and outside it; all things considered, one is wiser to order the specialties of the house and of the season, even in this day of deep-freeze wonders. There are, how-ever, a good many authentic Creole meat dishes, like *grillades*, which are veal rounds simmered in a tightly covered iron pot over a slow fire in a mixture of their own juices, a butter-and-flour *roux*, and the familiar tomato-green pepper-onion-garlic-parsley combination. They are wonderfully tender and flavorsome, and at no restaurant in New Orleans are they better than at Arnaud's. Another local specialty is *bouilli*, a beef brisket which is served with a horseradish sauce to-gether with a few of the vegetables with which it has been boiled: it sounds rather like a New England boiled dinner, but it does not taste like one—here again it is the seasoning that counts. *Bouilli* is a specialty at Tujague's, on Decatur Street, the only remaining Creole restaurant in New Orleans which serves a simple *table d'hôte* dinner; the menu seldom varies, and *bouilli* is usually to be found on it. Chicken is served in dozens of different ways—it is almost as indis-pensable as seafood. Chicken gumbo and jambalaya are everyday af-fairs; for more specialized dishes you should try the *poulet chanteclair* at Antoine's and Galatoire's chicken *à la bonne femme*. As for game, it is not readily obtainable at restaurants except at places like An-toine's, and then, of course, only in season (unless you are willing to settle for the frozen variety), and it has virtually disappeared from the markets. But if you should be so fortunate as to get hold of a few wild ducks there are some marvelous Creole recipes for preparing them—the strong flavor of game benefits from qualification with aromatic herbs and spices.

The great weakness of Creole cooking is its scarcity of desserts, and this is rather strange, considering their abundance in eighteenth century France—another emphatic proof of the distance between French and Louisiana cuisines. The only first-rate restaurant in New Orleans which serves a variety of really good desserts is Brennan's: Antoine's makes a superb chocolate soufflé and Galatoire's *coupe Princesse* is not lightly to be scorned; *crêpes Suzette* and *baba au rhum* are fairly common—so are caramel custard and *bananes flam-bées;* but one looks in vain for the flaky pastries, the *meringue glacée*, and the light and delectable mousses which characterize authentic French cookery—even the pie Saint-Honoré, a beautiful fluffy affair one used to see in all the bake shops, is beginning to disappear. (There is one excellent bakery which does specialize in French pastries, the Pâtisserie aux Quatre Saisons on St. Peter Street, with a branch on Royal.) The reason for this dearth may be that Creole cooking is so very heavy that ambitious desserts are simply not in order—and yet this is perhaps not the reason after all, for chocolate soufflé, *bananes flambées*, and *crêpes Suzette* could scarcely be termed light, and are certainly ambitious enough in their way.

The Creoles customarily drank wine with their meals—those who could afford to, that is, for before the development of the California vineyards the wine had to be imported and was therefore relatively expensive. For some reason claret and sauterne have always been the most popular wines in New Orleans: the local taste does not seem to favor extremely dry beverages; the favorite cocktails, too (like the Sazerac), are on the sweet side, and when a native mixes an Old Fashioned or a Manhattan he will frequently add just a touch of herbsaint, which is an absinthe substitute with a sweet, licorice-like flavor. Cocktails are said to have originated in New Orleans, and their inventor is supposed to have been a druggist named Peychaud, who operated a pharmacy at 437 Royal Street. According to Stanley Clisby Arthur, the first cocktail was a mixture of sugar, cognac, and bitters (which M. Peychaud manufactured), and the word represents an American corruption of the French *coquetier*, the egg-shaped cup from which the beverage was sipped. Wine drinking is no longer very common in the city; the great middle-class beverage now is beer, here as elsewhere. Many well-to-do families, however, continue to serve wine with both lunch and dinner, and of course the wineheads around Lafayette Square consume enormous quantities of cheap port, muscatel, and sherry.

Everyone drinks coffee. Most of the natives still prefer it mixed with chicory in a proportion of seven or eight parts of the former to two or three of the latter, but pure coffee is becoming increasingly popular: ten years ago a waitress would ask you which you wanted; now she assumes, unless you tell her differently, that you prefer the pure. New Orleanians like a dark roast, they make it very strong (two tablespoons to a cup), they like to drip it, and they usually drink it black except at breakfast: the traditional way to serve *café au lait* is to pour coffee and hot milk, simultaneously and in equal parts, into a mug thick enough to retain the heat. (The Café du Monde in the French Market serves it in this manner, together with Creole doughnuts.) On special occasions, *café brûlot* (also known as *café Diable*) is served instead of the ordinary after-dinner demitasse; this is a potent and highly dramatic concoction made by placing cognac, orange and lemon peel, sugar, allspice, cloves, and cinnamon in a silver dish and, as the cookbooks say, "igniting the whole." Coffee is then added, and while the mixture is still flaming it is stirred with a silver ladle. After a few brief moments (so that there will be some alcohol left!), the flames are extinguished, and the *brûlot* is poured into coffee cups of special size and shape. It is traditional for the lights to be turned out while this drink is being prepared, so that the glamorous blue flames will show to best advantage—this is done even in the big restaurants, for it is good advertising also. Another exciting after-dinner drink is orange *brûlot*. This is made by taking a large orange and slitting the skin around its middle; the peel is then forced off the fruit so that it forms a cup in which brandy, sugar, and allspice are burned together: the *brûlot* is then drunk from the cup. This drink gives off a delightful aroma when burning, for the fragrance of the oil in the orange skin blends with that of the brandy.

One is almost as embarrassed at choosing among the restaurants in New Orleans as among the houses or the courtyards; there are so many good ones. Antoine's and Galatoire's continue to head the list, probably, and are very different from each other: the former is huge, with a labyrinth of dimly lighted private rooms that remind you a bit of the Lapérouse; Galatoire's is tiny and as brightly lighted as a barbershop, which in fact it rather resembles—the jewels of the women glitter as brilliantly as in a jeweler's window. I personally feel more at ease in Galatoire's (Antoine's is a bit overwhelming), but the service in both is flawless. I am tempted to place Brennan's, a relative newcomer among New Orleans restaurants, third on my list. It was founded by the late Owen Brennan in the forties, and was located for several years on Bourbon Street, in the building previously occupied by the old Vieux Carré Restaurant; now it has moved into the spacious old Faurie mansion, one of the most beautiful houses on Royal Street, which for many years had been operated as a restaurant known as the Patio Royal. Brennan's has flourished in its new setting: there was a certain confusion caused by the expansion of its staff and adjustment to the new surroundings; for a while the service suffered, but now it is back to normal, and the food has always been very, very good. It is not the least pretentious restaurant in New Orleans, but it also has a genuine elegance, and the prices are very reasonable: it is certainly the only place of its kind in America where you can drink a luncheon cocktail—and a good one, too—for twenty-five cents. (When Brennan's started this institution there was a flurry of alarm in New Orleans restaurants, some of which now have imitated it.) Brennan's is the most popular luncheon spot in the French Quarter, and there is apt to be a crowd in the evening, too. It is to be hoped that the quality of the food and service will not suffer as a result of all this business; as far as I can tell, there have been no signs of it as yet.

Arnaud's is a restaurant which, like Galatoire's, has always been as popular with the natives as with the tourists—a good sign that the food can be depended upon to be authentic. It is a large place, and, like Brennan's, does a big business. It has a long menu, perhaps the longest in town, and an excellent cellar; the service, however, leaves a good bit to be desired. Broussard's little restaurant on Conti Street is very pleasant in the summer—there is a charming court where you can dine *al fresco*—but in the winter you must sit indoors and look at the murals, which are dreadful. Tujague's, on Decatur across from the French Market, serves an excellent and very reasonable Creole *table d'hôte*—the portions are small, but presently, as course follows course, you begin to see why.

Outside the French Quarter, Dunbar's (formerly Corinne Dunbar's) is probably the best restaurant in New Orleans serving Creole cuisine; there are some who rank it with Antoine's and Galatoire's, and I confess that each time I revisit this elegant little establishment I am tempted to agree with them. Dunbar's is located in one of the old mansions on St. Charles Avenue, and you must make a reservation in advance. The dinner is *table d'hôte*, with a limited choice of entrées, and the food is such as you would be served in the very finest Creole homes in New Orleans. There is only one dining room and a parlor where you may have a cocktail before you are ushered into it: the atmosphere is intimate without being informal. The colored servants wear white gloves, the china and silver are of the very finest, and the dishes come to the table beautifully garnished. Dunbar's clientele is composed largely of New Orleanians; tourists never seem to know about it.

Maylie's, on Poydras Street, is a restaurant in which I have never been disappointed. It serves a family-style Creole dinner, as do Tujague's and Dunbar's, and it is that rarest of all things in New Orleans —a good, low-priced restaurant which is never crowded. (Why this should be so I have never understood, for it is only a matter of four or five blocks from the heart of the business district.) Planted in the hallway of Maylie's is a gigantic wistaria vine, nearly a century old; its central stem, as big around as a tree trunk, pushes right up through the roof of the building.

Commander's Palace, in the Garden District, is, like Dunbar's, located in an old private home; it is larger and less formal, though, and is very popular with natives and tourists alike. Commander's has a reputation for seasoning everything very highly—a reputation, I should say, which is well earned—but its stuffed flounder is about as good as any you will find in the city, and it holds exclusive rights to a memorable soft-shell turtle stew.

"The only thing that can be said against eating," said gastronome Frank Schloesser, "is that it takes away one's appetite." When I have to leave New Orleans, I sometimes think the only thing that can be said against the food there is that it takes away one's appetite for what is commonly called food in most American cities.

The Music

THERE is not much of it left—of the kind, that is, which people think of as New Orleans music (by which is meant the kind of jazz that became popular here around the turn of the century). Some, but not much. The jazz devotee who comes to the city looking for the little four- or five-piece Negro combos which used to improvise gloriously in the Basin Street brothels and honky-tonks will get a real shock: Basin Street today is a characterless thoroughfare lined partly with garages and parking lots, partly with a low-cost Negro housing project; there is not a single bar or honky-tonk on it. The street received its death blow in 1917, when Mayor Behrman closed down Storyville, the notorious red-light district, because of pressure from the United States Navy.

The only places where you will be likely to hear authentic Dixieland jazz today are in the French Quarter—on Bourbon Street, mostly, which inherited something of the character of Storyville. And it is authentic only by comparison with the sort of jazz which you can hear anywhere else: the day of the Negro musicians who played only by ear and whose group rapport was nothing short of supernatural is gone forever—as are most of the musicians themselves, who now belong almost as thoroughly to the past as the strolling minstrels of the thirteenth century. This is not to say that some small and very good Negro combos no longer exist in the city; they do, but their specialty is not Dixieland—jazz has traveled a long way in the sixty-odd years of its existence, and the style of the modern musicians (all of whom, by the way, can read music and many of whom learned to play their instruments in school) reflects all the influences of the latter-day jazz tradition: boogiewoogie, swing, bop, and "progressive." There is a conscious artistry about their performance that is sometimes quite impressive, but it is a far cry from pioneer jazz. The New Orleans Negro has become sophisticated musically, as in other ways, and jazz is essentially a primitive business, which is why it is so very stirring. The tradition of marching to funerals to the slow, sweet, sad music of a jazz band (which as soon as the body was lowered into the grave struck up a lively, jubilant tune like "High Society") has all but disappeared among the local Negroes, together with many other customs which the younger generation among them regards as old fashioned.

New Orleans, as almost everyone knows, is the birthplace of jazz, and produced more talents in what is probably the truest of American art forms than any other city in the country: Buddy Bolden, Bunk Johnson, "Jelly Roll" Morton, "King" Oliver, "Kid" Ory, Sidney Bechet, Fate Marable, Louis Armstrong, "Papa" Celestin, and many, many others. But most of these men are dead, and Armstrong has not lived in New Orleans since 1922, the year he went to join "King" Oliver's band in Chicago. When "Papa" Celestin died, in 1956, the city lost its last remaining link with early jazz; he was the last of the old instrumentalists to remain on the local scene, and played magnificently at the Paddock Lounge on Bourbon Street until just before his death. "Papa" excelled in marching songs, and had arranged with Southland Records for a two-album recording of which only the first (" 'Papa' Celestin's Golden Wedding") was finished; his performance on this album of "Down by the Riverside" and "Oh Didn't He Ramble" are classics of their kind. As for singers, there is only one of them left, and that is Lizzie Miles, who performed until quite recently at the Mardi Gras Lounge and may still be heard occasionally at Tony Almerico's Sunday afternoon jam sessions on Royal Street.

Lizzie is an extraordinary woman. She was in Paris in the twenties, even before Josephine Baker, when American blues singers were at the peak of their popularity. At the little cabaret on the Rue Blanche in Montmartre where she appeared, as the program reads, "from midnight to breakfast," she was billed as the "Black Rose of White Street" and sang her numbers both in English and in her native Creole French. Lizzie grew up in New Orleans' Seventh Ward, which also produced Sidney Bechet and many other jazz pioneers, and she knew them all. The idiom with which she is most familiar is ragtime, and there is probably no singer alive today who can match her performance of "Salty Dog," "A Good Man Is Hard to Find," "The Darktown Strutters' Ball," and "Bill Bailey, Won't You Please Come Home?" (These may be heard on an album recently released by Capitol called "A Night in Old New Orleans.") Lizzie is in her sixties, but her heavy contralto is still smooth and powerful: what distinguishes her performance, however, is not so much her voice as her timing and her exuberance, particularly the latter, which has a way of matching (and occasionally, in the playful way known only to singers in small Negro combos, of competing with) such virile instruments as the trumpet and trombone: the Capitol album, with Sharkey at the trumpet and his little Dixieland band in the background, furnishes a good illustration of this masterly sort of give-and-take, impossible in large bands and very rare nowadays even in small ones.

The background which produced such artists as Lizzie Miles, Sidney Bechet, and Louis Armstrong was a colorful one. The Negro tribal dances in Congo Square, though discontinued during the Civil War, were resumed at its termination, and were still in progress when cornetist Buddy Bolden, the leader of the first jazz orchestra, was in his teens, and it was impossible for him and the other Negro musicians in the city to escape the influence of this primitive, "stomping" kind of music which, together with the popular song and the spiritual, constituted the only musical tradition in the city outside the conservatories, and none of these men could read a note of music. Before emancipation, the slaves had played on home-made instruments similar to those in Africa: on banjos, and on drums made from hollow logs and bamboo tubes; these last were known as *bamboulas*, and provided the Creole composer Louis Moreau Gottschalk, who had also witnessed the dances in Congo Square, with the title of one of his best-known works, based on these dances. They also used castanets fashioned from a pair of bones and a primitive rattle made by exposing the jawbone of an ass to dry in the sun, so that the teeth loosened and produced a rattling sound when struck. The earliest Negro instruments were thus strings and percussion, and both of these continued to play an important part in jazz bands until the 1920's, when the banjo was eliminated because of the increasing domination of powerful wind instruments.

Buddy Bolden was a barber by trade—he had a little shop on

Franklin (now Crozat) Street, in the Basin Street area—but he was known mainly for his music; even before the Spanish-American War his dance band had acquired the reputation of being the hottest in town. But Bolden did not limit himself to dance music. The Negro neighborhoods at the turn of the century were full of what were known as "Social Aid and Pleasure Clubs," each of which had a band which tried to outdo all the others on the occasions (which were frequent) when they paraded in the street and played at funerals: there were the Hobgoblins, the Buzzards, the Mysterious Babies, the Zulus, the Money Wasters, the Original Swells, the Diamond Swells, and many others. The pioneer jazz instrumentalists all participated in these processions—it was in the midst of one, on Labor Day, that Buddy Bolden went violently insane and had to be committed to the asylum where he spent the remainder of his days. His successor was Bunk Johnson, also a cornetist, and it was Johnson who persuaded Sidney Bechet, who was just learning the clarinet, to join his band, known as the Eagles.

Another important source of jazz was Storyville, for most jazz forms were developed, not on wind instruments but on the piano, and almost every brothel and honky-tonk in the red-light district was equipped with one. The pianists, who had had no formal musical education, had a rough, bouncing technique on the keys, which, under their fingers, sounded as if they were being dusted more or less haphazardly with a cloth—and it is thought that this may have been the origin of the term "ragtime." In this manner they played the popular songs of the day, and in this connection it is important to remember that jazz is mainly a matter of interpretation and technique: any music at all can be "jazzed up," including the most unlikely, such as hymns and funeral marches, and this is precisely what happened. But they also made up their own tunes, and these were usually "blues" (formally, a short theme of twelve-bar duration based on certain minor chords). The pianists also improvised the words: early jazz was essentially vocal, and nothing really happened to it when it was played on instruments, for the musicians simply continued to sing on these; that is, they played them in a singing style. (This similarity of vocal and instrumental styles is still a characteristic of jazz; it is most evident, perhaps, in the work of Louis Armstrong, whose voice and trumpet have the same basic phrasing.)

Storyville produced some very fine musicians—like "Jelly Roll" Morton, who played at Lulu White's elaborate brothel on Basin

Street. Sexuality was thus present in jazz from the beginning (to this day the Negroes in New Orleans use the word *jazz* as a verb to refer to the act of sexual intercourse), and the influence of the cribhouse is seen in two of its most important moods: the melancholy which is a product of frustrated idealism, and which reveals itself in the yearning, longing quality of early blues songs; and in the reckless gaiety of ragtime, which accompanies the satisfaction of a powerful, uncomplicated emotional urge.

Eventually the single singer at his piano was joined or replaced by a song specialist (like Lizzie Miles), and other instruments were added: the banjo, the trumpet, the clarinet, the trombone, and the drum. The banjo was an indispensable part of the early combo, for its natural role was to supply a background for the singer, and no jazz band was without its singer in those days. As time went on, these combos showed an increasing preference for ragtime over blues; boogiewoogie, which superseded ragtime, marked a return to the blues tradition at the same time that it restored the pianist to his original importance. This style combined blues with ragtime in a highly ingenious manner: the pianist kept the blues theme with one hand while with the other he doubled up the tempo, playing eight instead of four beats to the bar—the result was a fairly complicated type of music making considerable demands upon the technical skill of the pianist; and when one considers that some of the greatest performers of boogiewoogie were unable to read music one is moved to real admiration: the red-light district, as "Jelly Roll" has said, was full of "professors."

In the first decade of the century, New Orleans resounded with music—with Negro music, too, a thing which, now that jazz has become international, people tend to forget. White musicians at this time were playing either Chopin or sentimental popular songs, and the only original music of any consequence came from the Negro neighborhoods and the red-light district where they were employed. It seemed as if nothing could suppress the musical exuberance of the Negroes: if they couldn't afford store-bought instruments they would make their own, like their ancestors, and an ordinary washboard in the hands of such a performer as "Baby" Dodds, who slapped it with thimbles, could be a very effective percussion instrument. It was a climate out of which, musically, almost anything could come, and what came out of it was Dixieland.

Dixieland fused the various jazz traditions which had been developing in the Negro neighborhoods and in Storyville to the marching music of the street bands, which stressed the second and fourth beat of every measure: the strong beat was supplied by the drums and tuba, while the clarinet, the trombone, and the cornet wove a melody; the cornet played the lead, and the other two made up their own countermelodies. Thus was developed the polyphony which characterizes the best of Dixieland jazz and which, according to Frederic Ramsey, Jr., and Charles Edward Smith in *Jazzmen*, "in its more complex manifestations became a dissonant counterpoint that antedated Schoenberg." It is an enormously exciting kind of music, as anyone who has listened to Louis Armstrong playing "When the Saints Go Marching In" knows, and it was the last authentic jazz to come out of the city. When it was at its height, the police closed Storyville, an occasion which in itself furnished a subject for blues treatment:

> *I can't keep open, I'm gonna close up my shack.*
> *The chief of police done tore my playhouse down;*
> *No use in grievin', I'm gonna leave this town . . .*

It was the end of jazz in New Orleans. After that it went North with the Streckfus Line steamers, on which Fate Marable held forth with an orchestra which included "Baby" Dodds at the drums, "Pops" Foster at the string bass, and Johnny St. Cyr, the almost legendary master of the banjo-guitar. Armstrong joined them for a season, and finally, at "King" Oliver's invitation, settled in Chicago.

After that, jazz spread to the four winds, and many things happened to it: the saxophone was added, and the bands increased in size, which meant that the banjo had to be dropped—it simply couldn't be heard—and that the music had to be arranged so that the players wouldn't get in one another's way. Jazz was taken up by white musicians, and the new maestros, like Benny Goodman, brought a classical background to bear upon what was originally a primitive and spontaneous idiom: they smoothed out the music, substituting for the obvious accent on the second and fourth beat a more rolling type of rhythm; this happened in the mid-thirties, and the result was swing, so called because the music, instead of jumping heavily, swung lightly from bar to bar. It was wonderful to dance to, but something was lacking: when jazz became commercialized, and the big dance bands were in demand by hotels and college campuses all over the country, something of the joy went out of it—musicians came to regard their work as a job like any other, and the old jam sessions, where small Negro combos played together for the sheer love of playing even when all the customers had gone home, became increasingly rare. In the late thirties and early forties, a group of musicians in New York who had studied the modern composers developed bop, which introduced changes of harmony as well as of rhythm. The tendency to intellectualize jazz has recently reached its climax in what is commonly called "progressive" jazz, which in the hands of interpreters like Lee Konitz, Gerry Mulligan, and Dave Brubeck reveals such eclectic influences as Schoenberg, Bartók, and Berg. What began as simple marches has ended as chamber music.

Of course, it had to go somewhere; it couldn't remain static, and whether or not it has ended by ceasing to be jazz is largely a matter of definition. There are many who think that when it left New Orleans it lost its essential identity, and certainly the differences between "Papa" Celestin and Dave Brubeck are differences of kind rather than of degree. Two members of "Papa's" original band, incidentally, are still playing on at the Paddock Lounge: trombonist Bill Matthews and pianist Octave Crosby. Nowadays you can hear authentic Dixieland at two other places in New Orleans: at the Famous Door on Bourbon Street, and at the Parisian Room on Royal, where Tony Almerico holds a jam session every Sunday afternoon and where, if you are lucky, Lizzie Miles may drop in and sing "Salty Dog" if she is in the mood. Otherwise she won't, and that is the way jazz used to be.

The Cemeteries

The New Orleans cemeteries are little cities filled with miniature houses, for burials were all above ground until comparatively recent times, when the drainage problem was solved. You feel this particularly in the older cemeteries; the oldest of them all, St. Louis Number One, is truly a city of the dead—the tombs are constructed of the same materials as the old houses, cement over brick, sometimes with iron railings which enclose them as houses are enclosed, and you feel that the inhabitants have simply *moved*, that they have exchanged a larger house for a smaller one. The tombs are crowded together just like the old houses, and divided into blocks by straight paths exactly like the streets which Pauger laid out in the old city. There are neighborhoods, too, just as in the living one: in the older cemeteries the Protestants and Catholics are buried in separate areas, and though Negroes in New Orleans occupy the same cemeteries as whites there are certain zoning restrictions—segregation extends to the dead as well as to the living.

Because of this illusion you tend to think of the deceased as living (instead of merely lying) next door to one another, and the dates on the slabs which establish that the neighbors are often of different generations does not destroy the illusion: they are all members of the same community, a community that exists outside of time, where the accident and the tyranny of that dimension have no meaning. Here the dead have a reality lacking in cities where they are hidden beneath the earth's surface; when their houses are all around you it is not easy to forget them. The city of the dead seems

172

as real and as important as the living city, of which it appears to be merely the microcosm.

The very earliest burials were in the ground, in shallow graves which, when there were heavy rains, as often as not exposed their contents to the open air; it is for this reason that the oldest graves have all been destroyed (the oldest tombstone in St. Louis Number One dates from 1800) and that a law was passed early in the nineteenth century making burials above ground compulsory. During the yellow-fever and cholera epidemics this law was violated of necessity: people were dying at such a rate that the demand for tombs greatly exceeded the supply, and there were not even enough gravediggers to go around.

A typical New Orleans cemetery is enclosed by fairly high walls, whitewashed on the outside and thick enough to contain the length of a coffin: these wall tombs, which look like bakers' ovens, are for the poorer families and are usually rented for certain periods of time, after which, if the rent is not renewed, the coffins are burned and their contents either burned with them or buried anonymously in a common plot. "They bake their dead in ovens," an English tourist wrote home in 1847, "as we do our brown Johns for breakfast." Most of the older family tombs consist of two vaults, an upper and a lower: the coffin is sealed into the upper one for a length of time prescribed by law, after which it is removed and burned, while the bones are placed in the crypt below—in this way several generations can be accommodated in the same tomb.

"New Orleans has no architecture except that found in its cemeteries," said Mark Twain, who found the houses of the dead more impressive than the houses of the living; and the fact that the tombs here were all above ground certainly provided unusual opportunities for architects and sculptors. He was probably thinking of Washington Cemetery Number One, the Girod Street Cemetery (now no more) or St. Louis Number One, but all the older cemeteries in New Orleans are interesting from this point of view: one sees mausoleums of every possible shape and size, and the statuary with which they are adorned is evidence that the graveyard sculptors of the last century were frequently men of considerable skill and invention. When the old Girod Street Cemetery was abandoned several years ago, prior to demolition, a whole army of scavengers descended upon it after dark armed with chisels, hammers, and crowbars: marble obelisks and cherubs disappeared by the score, to find their way into antique shops and private homes, and more than one coffee table around town has for its top a curiously decorated slab from one of the old tombs.

The Girod Street Cemetery, which was the first Protestant burial ground in the city, presented a macabre appearance for many years before it was finally destroyed. Grave robbers had broken into the tombs, pried open the coffins in the hope of finding a diamond ring or a necklace, and left them lying in full view, their grisly contents exposed to the elements. The coffins were usually of the type favored by nineteenth century undertakers in New Orleans—iron, with a glass window through which one could view the face of the deceased, and with a surface corrugated (in the case of women and girls) to resemble folds of drapery: the effect was rather Egyptian.

A colony of hobos and wineheads used the Girod Street Cemetery for a camping ground, and it was a common thing to see empty bottles of muscatel and sherry lying about in the tall weeds with which the place was overgrown, and the charred remains of camp fires. Some of the larger, communal tombs, designed for the members of associations such as the Odd Fellows, Masons, and the like, provided ideal shelter in case of rain, and when the police raided the spot, which they sometimes did because of public pressure (it had become dangerous to walk through), it was an easy matter to crawl into one of the empty ovens and replace the slab from the inside so that it looked just like all the others. Grave robbery has always been a common occurrence in New Orleans, probably because tombs which are above ground are easily broken into, and this is one reason why the walls are so high, with big iron gates that are locked after dark; yet, in spite of these precautions, there is not a cemetery in the city that has not suffered depredations of this type.

The oldest cemetery in New Orleans, St. Louis Number One, on Basin Street between St. Louis and Toulouse, is the remnant of a burial ground which originally included a far greater area, and many of the famous old Creole families are buried here. The tombs are crowded quite close together; some are pyramidal, others circular, but the favorite form is a cube with a neoclassic pediment. Some of them are surrounded by iron fences; others are decorated with miniature iron balconies and crosses. The area is treeless, for in such a small space roots would unsettle the tombs and the walls; the ground is so soft anyway that some of the mausoleums lean at crazy angles, while the bottom row of vaults on the Basin Street wall has sunk so low that no more burials can be made in them. Some tombs are badly cracked, and ferns and even miniature shrubs have taken root on them: spiders and lizards are everywhere. Many of the inscriptions, of course, are in French, and you can see the epitaph "Killed in a Duel" again and again.

Etienne de Boré is buried here, in the same mausoleum with his grandson, the historian Charles Gayarré; so are Bernard Marigny de Mandeville, Paul Morphy, and Marie Laveau, Queen of the Voodoos (though a tradition persists which identifies as hers an unmarked oven in St. Louis Number Two). One is struck by the simplicity of these early nineteenth century tombs: there is nothing about them to suggest the former wealth of their occupants. De Boré and Marigny were very rich men, and had they died half a century later you would expect their graves to be distinguished by a certain ornateness, like the ones in Metairie Cemetery. Governor Claiborne buried both of his wives here: Eliza Lewis, who died in 1804, at the age of twenty-one, and Clarice Duralde, whom he married two years later and who died of yellow fever in 1809, also aged twenty-one. Eliza's tomb is in the Protestant section of the cemetery, Clarice's in the Catholic. On both tombs the governor caused the following ambiguous inscription to be carved: "For the virtuous there is a happier and better world." Eliza's brother, Micajah, who was Claiborne's secretary, followed her here a year later; he was killed in a duel defending his sister's reputation, which had been attacked by enemies of the governor. Claiborne himself was buried beside his second wife until 1906, when his remains were taken to Metairie. You should also notice the large circular mausoleum of the Italian Mutual and Benevolent Society. The idea for this tomb belonged to a citizen named I. T. Barelli, who imported Piero Gualdi, an Italian sculptor, to build it. Ironically, the first man to be buried in it was its builder, Gualdi, and the second was Barelli.

St. Louis Number Two, at North Claiborne and Bienville, is larger but less picturesque, with not so much ironwork and statuary. It was built in 1822, and contains the graves of Dominique You, the reformed pirate who became a ward leader in the city; Alexander Milne, founder of Milneburg; and Oscar J. Dunn, the mulatto lieutenant-governor of Louisiana during Henry Clay Warmoth's Reconstruction administration.

St. Louis Number Three, near the end of Esplanade Avenue, is the largest but the least interesting of the trio bearing that name: it stands on the site of an old leper colony established by Governor Miró in the eighteenth century. Called Bayou Cemetery for many years, it was acquired by the St. Louis Cathedral in 1856. It does have trees and shrubbery (space not being at such a premium in this part of the city), but it is untypical of the older New Orleans cemeteries in that it is not enclosed within brick walls. There is a big monument by James Gallier, Jr., in memory of his father, who was lost with his wife at sea in the wreck of the *Evening Star* in 1866.

St. Vincent de Paul Cemetery, on Louisa Street, was once owned by Pepe Lulla, one of the most famous swordsmen in New Orleans, whose victims were supposedly so numerous that, according to tradition, he was obliged to start a cemetery in order to dispose of their bodies. Actually, St. Vincent de Paul's had already been in operation when Lulla acquired it shortly before the Civil War; he is himself buried there, having died in 1888 at the age of seventy-two. There is an interesting pattern on the exterior of the brick walls surrounding this cemetery.

The best-designed cemetery in New Orleans is St. Roch's, at St. Roch and Derbigny, which is modeled after the Campo Santo dei Tedeschi in Rome. It was founded by Father Peter Thevis, a young German priest who, at the height of the yellow-fever epidemic in 1868, prayed to St. Roch (patron saint of plague sufferers in the Middle Ages) for divine intervention, promising to build with his own hands a chapel in his honor. When the epidemic subsided, Father Thevis kept his word, and the chapel stands today at the far end of the cemetery, facing the entrance gate. It is tiny and very beautiful—one of the architectural jewels of the city, really, with a vaulted ceiling so lovely you almost wish Father Thevis (who lies buried at the foot of the altar) had changed his calling and produced others like it. The shrine enjoys a local reputation for miraculous cures, as is testified by the little room on the right of the chapel, which is filled with artificial limbs and crutches.

St. Roch's looks like a fortress, a little medieval walled city of the dead. It is unusually symmetrical, the balance being achieved by the position of the chapel and towering entrance gate, which face each other at either end, and by a series of chapel-like niches in each of the walls and at the four corners depicting the Stations of the Cross. This cemetery was apparently popular with the German colony here, for a great many of the inscriptions are in that language.

Cypress Grove, one of a cluster of cemeteries at the extreme end of Canal Street, is the best-planted burial ground in the city. (In spite of its name, the trees are mostly oaks and magnolias.) There is some

DETAIL, CYPRESS GROVE CEMETERY

CYPRESS GROVE CEMETERY

unusual sculpture here, too, like the grotesque iron dolphins with human faces on the Leeds tomb to the right of the entrance; the entrance gate itself shows Egyptian influence. William Mumford, executed by General Butler for tearing down a Federal flag in 1862, was buried for many years in the Canal Street wall, in an oven ignominiously marked "Grave of Mumford"; the body was recently removed to Greenwood Cemetery, across the street, where it rests in a mausoleum containing more than six hundred Confederate soldiers.

The melting-pot character of New Orleans in the nineteenth century is nowhere more evident than in its cemeteries. The inscriptions are in all languages, and here in Cypress Grove there is even a Chinese mausoleum, a communal affair owned by local tongs which bury their members here temporarily pending shipment to their native land: every ten years or so the vaults are opened, and the bones are removed and placed in the steel boxes in which they are returned to China. The purpose of the grate in the corner of the mausoleum is to burn incense during funeral services.

Lafayette Cemetery Number One, on Washington Avenue and Sixth Street, is a well planned and well planted burial ground with the slightly autocratic air appropriate to its location in the heart of the Garden District. Many yellow-fever victims were buried here (the epidemic raged with particular violence in this part of town), and it is not unusual to see a tombstone which records the death of a whole family in the space of a single week. Lately there have been evidences of vandalism in this cemetery: a number of slabs have been cracked and broken, exposing bones and coffins to the public view.

Biggest of all the New Orleans cemeteries is the one in Metairie. Originally a race track, it was converted into a burial ground in the 1870's and is thus relatively modern; burials here are below ground as well as above, for the land is high and comparatively dry, so that Metairie lacks the built-up look of the older cemeteries and is coming more and more to resemble those in other cities. It is an enormous place, and a regular maze: you can wander about in it for hours looking for a particular tomb, in spite of the printed maps with which the management thoughtfully provides you. Even in a car (you can drive up and down the spacious avenues) it is easy to get lost, and if you park your car somewhere you may never find it again unless, like Theseus in the Minotaur's labyrinth, you use a string.

Metairie Cemetery has many tombs which reflect the ostentation of the late nineteenth century, and it is full of dubious statuary—allegorical female figures and angels tapping on the doors of tombs to awaken their occupants to eternal life—but there are also many of great beauty and dignity. General John Bell Hood's tomb is here, though finding it is another matter, and General Beauregard is buried in the big mausoleum of the Louisiana Division of the Army of Tennessee. The tombs of Governors Claiborne and Warmoth are also in Metairie.

There is one day in the year when all these cities of the dead are decorated almost as brilliantly as is the living city at Mardi Gras, and that is All Saints' Day on November 1st—not, as in most Catholic communities, on All Souls' Day, which is November 2nd. It is one of the most important holidays in the city for Catholics and Protestants alike: for a week or so in advance the cemeteries are filled with people putting the tombs in proper order—whitewashing them, painting the iron railings, and weeding and mowing the plots. Early on the morning of All Saints' Day they return, laden with flowers and wreaths, real and artificial, with which they deck the graves. (Chrysanthemums are the favorite flowers, and the local nurseries have made a big business of growing them just for this purpose.) It is a point of prestige with New Orleans families to clean and decorate the graves of their deceased on this occasion: one hears approving comments, and an occasional disparaging one, on all sides, and it is as natural for many citizens to spend this day in the cemetery, admiring the tombs, as it is for them to spend every other day outside it; some bring their lunches with them, and whole families will be seen picnicking among the graves. It is not uncommon for New Orleanians, seeing an undecorated tomb, to leave a few flowers on it, for there is always something a little indecent about a bare grave on All Saints' Day.

There is nothing at all solemn about All Saints' Day in New Orleans; on the contrary, a holiday atmosphere prevails in all the cemeteries: balloons, peanuts, hot dogs, ice cream, and cold drinks are sold at the entrances, exactly as at Mardi Gras, and until quite recently gumbo and hot coffee were dispensed at St. Vincent de Paul's. With the addition of outsiders to the city's population in recent years and the cultural leveling which accompanies increased transportation and communication facilities, All Saints' Day is beginning to lose some of its significance. But there are still enough natives around to keep the florists busy.

The Negroes

One out of every four of the city's inhabitants is colored. Full-blooded Negroes, however, are very rare, appearances to the contrary, for miscegenation with European and Indian stock was common from the very earliest slaveowning days. In New Orleans, mulattoes had always enjoyed special privileges: they were called *gens de couleur* rather than *nègres*, and Bienville's *Code Noir* prohibited them from marrying Negro slaves. They were themselves free, and when a white man had a child by a Negro slave he customarily freed the mother so that the child would be free likewise.

Through marriage within their own class and concubinage with whites, the number of *gens de couleur* in the city increased rapidly, jumping from thirty-one in 1769 to seventeen hundred in 1789. Some of them amassed large fortunes as plantation owners, merchants, and brokers, and sent their children abroad to be educated; others became shoemakers, upholsterers, masons, barbers, tailors, and carpenters—trades, incidentally, with which they are still locally identified, though Jim Crow legislation in the early 1900's, which did not distinguish between Negroes and mulattoes, outlawed colored barbers for white men. In the Battle of New Orleans, in 1815, the free men of color served with especial distinction, and during the Reconstruction they furnished some of the more intelligent and better-educated officeholders, like Oscar J. Dunn, who was lieutenant-governor of Louisiana.

This class, perhaps more numerous in New Orleans than in any other Southern city, did not come to be equated socially and politically with "full-blooded" Negroes until more than half a century

179

after the Civil War, with the advent of Jim Crowism; after that, the destiny of the "colored" man became inseparable from that of his darker brother. And what is not ordinarily realized is that for thirty-odd years following Reconstruction, Negroes of all gradations of color continued to associate freely with white men on terms as equal as those prevailing in other sections of the country. Jim Crowism was not, as C. Vann Woodward has recently shown in his *Strange Career of Jim Crow*, a necessary reaction against the evils of Reconstruction; other more liberal alternatives existed and were advocated with considerable energy by many Southern leaders. This was true especially in Louisiana, in spite of the fact that it was one of the last states to recover its freedom from Reconstruction administration: George Washington Cable was an outspoken liberalist, and Francis T. Nicholls, first of the post-Reconstruction governors, even made a few Negro appointments, as he tells in his autobiography: "After I was recognized as Governor, I set myself earnestly to work to bring about good feeling and confidence between the races. . . . I was particularly anxious by kindness and strict justice and impartiality to the colored people . . . that they should feel that they were not proscribed and to this end appointed a number of them to small offices sandwiching them on Boards between white men."

Unfortunately, racism triumphed. Negroes were disfranchised by property and educational qualifications and by a prohibitive poll tax (in 1904 there were only 1,342 registered Negro voters in Louisiana as against 130,334 in 1896), and segregation was applied to street cars and railroad coaches, to waiting rooms in railway stations, to water fountains, to toilets, and to many other public facilities. In New Orleans persons of either race were required to obtain consent of the majority of the inhabitants of a given area before they could move into it, and white and Negro prostitutes were segregated into separate districts. The application of these laws to the large in-between group which had hitherto enjoyed many white privileges was particularly productive of suffering, and while New Orleans has been fortunate in having a relatively enlightened colored population, the individuals involved have been anything but fortunate.

Since the early 1900's, the Negro in New Orleans, as elsewhere in the South, has struggled to free himself from these humiliating conditions: he has fought with dignity, with intelligence, with energy, and with the wonderful patience which is one of the strongest weapons of minority groups everywhere. For a while it looked as though he was fighting in vain. The First World War, in which more than 360,000 American Negroes saw military service, might have been expected to advance the cause of integration; instead, it was followed by a wave of unprecedented racial violence that swept the whole nation, the worst demonstrations occurring in Chicago; and the Jim Crow laws, rather than relaxing, became more stringent and more numerous.

Not until the thirties, when Negroes and whites again faced a common enemy in the form of the Depression, was there a significant improvement in the situation. The New Deal opened up a good many opportunities to Negroes, and World War II awakened the national conscience to the paradox that while we were avowedly fighting racism in Germany we were endorsing it at home, and to the irony of the fact that although Negroes were effectively barred from Southern polls they were by no means overlooked by the draft boards. The first definite step toward integration occurred shortly after the war, when the Southern states relaxed their qualifications for suffrage: as a result of this, the number of Negro registrants in Louisiana jumped from 1,672 in 1948 to 108,724 in 1952. Another important victory was gained when Negroes began to be admitted to the graduate schools of large Southern universities, a step which was justified on the ground that advanced instruction and facilities were unobtainable in Negro institutions. (For several years Negro graduate students have been permitted to register at Louisiana State University, and little or no friction has resulted.) Undergraduate admission has met with more resistance, the segregationists arguing that adequate opportunities at this level exist for Negroes in their own colleges, but in 1958 several Negro undergraduates entered Louisiana State University.

In July, 1948, President Truman ended segregation in the armed forces, a thing which had not been considered even by the most ardent reformers of the Reconstruction era (who, incidentally, overlooked a good many stains on their own carpet). This was a more far-reaching measure than it appeared to be on the surface, for it not only affected a large part of the population—and that among the most youthful and vigorous of its members—but it also proved to Southern whites that it was possible for them to live comfortably at close quarters on equal terms with Negro conscripts at the same time that it allowed Negro soldiers from the South a taste of integration which they could hardly be expected to forget the moment they returned to civilian life. More important still was the decision of the United States Supreme Court on May 17, 1954, that segregation in the public schools was unconstitutional, reversing a previous decision (in the *Plessy vs. Ferguson* case in 1896) which held that separation is not incompatible with equality. This decision affected immediately only the five districts represented by the Negro plaintiffs, but it was accompanied by an order that integration should become effective within a reasonable period of time throughout the South, and it met with considerable resistance. Many Southern communities immediately undertook the improvement of Negro schools and the construction of new ones that were as impressive physically as white schools, hoping in this way to prevent or delay enforcement of the order, but in so doing they were proceeding on the "separate but equal" proposition that had been outlawed by the Supreme Court, which specifically ruled that "in the field of public education the doctrine of separate but equal has no place" and that "separate educational facilities are inherently unequal."

In some states, integration has been accomplished in the public schools with a minimum of friction; in others it has occasioned temporary demonstrations; but in a few cases the schools have been closed indefinitely: the notorious incidents at Little Rock in 1957 and 1958 provide a precedent which a number of other Southern communities have shown an inclination to imitate. Controversy had centered previously mainly on what constituted a "reasonable" period of time, but Arkansas's Governor Orval Faubus, raising the issue of states' rights, openly challenged the authority of the Supreme Court to decide matters of this nature, and that he has the majority of public feeling behind him in Arkansas is only too apparent from the fact of his recent reelection: it has even been charged that, lacking any personal convictions on the issue, he deliberately exploited it for a political purpose. In a number of other Southern states the "reasonable" period of time allotted for white citizens to accustom themselves to the idea of integration has been spent by them in devising means to postpone compliance with the order.

Louisiana, unfortunately, has not proved precisely a pioneer in the advancement of Negro rights. Prejudice and fear are here, as elsewhere, the main deterrents, but while the former is primarily the property of uneducated whites the latter is shared by whites of all degrees of intelligence and education. Negroes compose more than a third of the state's population, and outnumber the whites in seventeen parishes. The white man is frankly fearful for his economy should the level of Negro education reach that of his own; he realizes that equal educational opportunities are now the only weapon which the Negro lacks, and this is why he is reluctant to place it in his hands. So far from feeling (as he sometimes maintains) that the Negro is not "ready" for equal education, he knows that he is, and the knowledge frightens him: if he were really convinced that Negroes would not profit from the opportunity, integration would proceed at a much faster rate. As William Faulkner recently observed: "That's what the white man in the South is afraid of: that the Negro, who has done so much with no chance, might do so much more with an equal one."

In New Orleans, school facilities on all levels for Negroes have compared favorably with those in other Southern cities. One of the benefits of Reconstruction was that it advanced the cause of Negro education: the first Negro university in the city (New Orleans University) was founded in 1869. There are at present two large Negro institutions of higher learning in New Orleans: Dillard University, in Gentilly, and Xavier University, on Pine Street, which is the only all-Negro Catholic university in the United States. The elementary and high schools are unusually well equipped, and perhaps this is one reason why there has been less agitation for an integrated school system here than in certain other cities. As yet there has been no attempt to enroll Negroes in the primary and secondary schools of New Orleans, but it is in the offing, and the city, realizing its imminence, has begun the process of preparation by relaxing certain Jim Crow restrictions, such as the one separating Negroes from whites on the local buses and street cars: this was accomplished overnight, with no advance publicity which might have provided an opportunity for organized demonstrations, and as a result there were no "incidents"—in a matter of weeks, both races adjusted to the situation.

There is less reason to believe that integration in the public schools could be accomplished as easily—a certain amount of publicity is inevitable here—but there is good reason to believe that the New Orleans public will prefer integration to the alternative of closing down the public schools; it is also unlikely that the local public will tolerate integration only if it is enforced, as at Little Rock, at the point of the bayonet. There are two important forces operating in favor of integration in New Orleans: one is the tolerance which the city comes by naturally as a result of its Latin heritage, and the other is religion, particularly the Roman Catholic religion, of which New Orleans is a stronghold: Archbishop Rummel has been particularly outspoken on the subject of classroom integration.

The Negro in New Orleans has scored many important victories in the last few years—even ten years ago many of the rights he now takes for granted did not exist—but discrimination is still the rule rather than the exception. It invades every area of human activity, not excluding the courtroom, though a Negro probably stands a better chance of receiving justice here than elsewhere in the state, and miscarriages of justice are by no means limited to Negroes: as Robert Penn Warren puts it, "It will be a happy day for the South when no court discriminates in its dealings between the Negro and the white man, just as it will be a happy day for the nation when no court discriminates between the rich man and the poor man."

The typical New Orleans Negro is not a malcontent, agitating fanatically for overnight equality: he is realistic, and he has waited so long for his rights that another two or three years are not going to make a great deal of difference to him; he is prepared to wait longer than that if need be. There is little bitterness in his attitude toward the white man; Negroes and whites have lived side by side in the French Quarter as well as in other neighborhoods in complete harmony, and there has been no violence here involving the racial question since the riot of 1895, where it figured only indirectly—a record of which many cities north of the Ohio River are unable to boast.

But he is a little tired of being considered "picturesque" and "colorful," and he is beginning to resent his traditional role as target for the white man's humor. I think you cannot blame him for this: it is difficult to take seriously someone at whom you have just laughed, and the Negro wants more than anything else to be taken seriously by the white man. New Orleans Negroes are becoming increasingly sensitive on this score: the marching bands (in which there was always a large comic element) have virtually disappeared from the city, and the Carnival parade of the Zulus becomes each year a somewhat soberer affair. Ten years ago there were several drugstores in the Negro neighborhoods where one could buy Voodoo charms and medicines, such as "Boss-fix" and "attraction" powders and special candles for special purposes; now there is only one of these, to my knowledge (the Cracker Jack Pharmacy on South Rampart Street), and the last time I entered it I was regarded by the proprietor with evident suspicion.

The fact—and it ought to be a welcome one—must be faced: the New Orleans Negro has changed. He is no longer the simple primitive that excited the admiration of Lafcadio Hearn nor the gentle smokehouse ornament that excited the sympathy of George Washington Cable. He is a citizen who pays taxes and answers the draft call, and where is the logic that requires he shall do these things without sharing in the benefits that result from them? Moreover, Negroes are beginning to swell the professional classes of the city, and it cannot be charged that they have practiced in their respective fields with anything less than distinction.

The white man in New Orleans must accept the challenge to his economy; it ought, in any case, to be no greater than the challenge to his conscience. And it is easy to exaggerate the economic threat: New Orleans has much to gain, as does the entire South, from the advancement of this large element of its population, which constitutes a vast reservoir of potential wealth and intelligence. It is significant that in at least one important cultural area where the lack of formal education is not a handicap the New Orleans Negro has achieved international reputation: I am thinking, of course, of music, and more specifically of the only original music to come out of the New World, which is jazz.

There is reason to believe that the New Orleans Negro, after nearly a century of qualified but gradually increasing freedom, is equal to the responsibilities which devolve upon a citizen in a democratic government. The real question is whether or not his white neighbor is equal to them—it is the white man, not the Negro, who is now on trial; and this is a question which should be answered very shortly.